The landscape of contemporary evangelical Christianity is a complex one, but in Tom Breen it has an excellent, entertaining tour guide, especially if you find concepts like "humility" and "facts" and "necessary footnotes" to be mere annoyances in the way of good writing. Swat those gnats aside, put on a Christian t-shirt, and enjoy the brilliance.

> — Jason Boyett, *author of* Pocket Guide to the Bible *and* Pocket Guide to the Apocalypse

You will laugh aloud at this satirical "bookumentary" about the unfortunate pop cultural unions between Jesus and the Christian's spiritual need to build a "God brand." *The Messiah Formerly Known as Jesus* is not only hilarious entertainment, but surprisingly insightful, as well.

> — Matthew Paul Turner, *author of* The Christian Culture Survival Guide, Hokey Pokey: Curious People Finding What Life's All About, *and the forthcoming* Churched

Tom Breen may be to serious theological discourse what Wikipedia is to reference works edited by guys who don't live with their moms, but he's a lot more fun to consult than, say, Boniface Wimmer (whose name I totally just got from Wikipedia—thanks, Tom!).

> — Andrew Beaujon, *author of* Body Piercing Saved My Life: Inside the Phenomenon of Christian Rock

Advance Praise for *The Messiah Formerly Known as Jesus*

Thanks be to Breen for his clarity in *The Messiah Formerly Known as Jesus*. If only I'd had it in the 4th century, the Council of Nicea would have featured much less shouting.

> — Arius, troublesome heretic

After reading this book, I can't believe that I'm the theologian who gets the nickname "Dumb Ox."

> — St. Thomas Aquinas, angelic doctor

The most profound work of theology since Bob Dylan's born-again albums. Only quibble is that my quotes are attributed to professional wrestlers.

—Origen, non-grappling exegete

Through the inscrutable designs of God, some are irretrievably damned and others vouchsafed Paradise. All, however, are predestined to get a good chuckle out of this book.

—John Calvin, lawyer and theologian

This book should have been nailed to the door of Wittenberg Cathedral. That way, people could have seen how smart I am by comparison.

—Martin Luther, church door vandal

Finally . . . a book about me . . .

—Jesus

Here's a book that should be laughed at . . .

—King James

THE MESSIAH FORMERLY KNOWN AS JESUS

THE MESSIAH FORMERLY KNOWN AS JESUS

Dispatches from the Intersection of Christianity and Pop Culture

Tom Breen

BAYLOR UNIVERSITY PRESS

Cover Design by Matthew Greenblatt, CenterPointe Design
Book Design by Ellen Condict

Library of Congress Cataloging-in-Publication Data

Breen, Tom.
    The Messiah formerly known as Jesus : dispatches from the
intersection of Christianity and pop culture / Tom Breen.
        p. cm.
    ISBN 978-1-60258-019-0 (pbk. : alk. paper)
    1. Christianity and culture. 2. Popular culture--Religious
aspects--Christianity. I. Title.

    BR115.C8B74 2007
    261.0973--dc22
                                                2007039747

Printed in the United States of America on acid-free paper
with a minimum of 30% pcw recycled content.

To John and Dan Breen, a pair of genuine scholars and honest-to-goodness Christians.

CONTENTS

ACKNOWLEDGMENTS

It would be odd to write a book like this and not start by acknowledging God, while at the same time appealing to his well-known capacity for mercy. In addition, I invoked the intercession of St. John, patron of writers, numerous times during the course of this project. And speaking of saintly intercession, the extent to which this work is worthwhile is largely due to the efforts of Casey Blaine, my editor at Baylor University Press—without her, this would have been a random stew of posts largely unnoticed in a murky corner of the Internet. Indeed, the whole crew at Baylor University Press has been nothing less than wonderful. Also deserving of special mention is the staff at *The Christian Century*, particularly Jason Byasee and David Heim, who first saw some lasting merit in the disjointed ramblings of the Internet Theologian. I leave it to posterity to judge whether they were misguided, but I certainly appreciate their publishing the article that led to this book. In addition to those noble folk, this work was written with the input and feedback of numerous insightful friends. In particular, I'm indebted to Phil Deslippe and Joe Pastula for being boon companions in exploring the fascinating contours of American religion. Mike Kirk and Marc Hatfield, the two funniest men I know, provided me with valuable guidance on the humorous tone of the book, warning me at key junctures where it could have started to resemble a work of actual scholarship. For similar advice, and for support too selfless to detail here, I am also grateful to Christine McCluskey. Plaudits must also go to my colleagues and coworkers, first at the *Journal Inquirer* and now at the *Associated Press*. In particular, I am grateful to Keith Phaneuf and Shaya Tayefe Mohajer for sharing their insights about this project and religion in general. I am especially grateful to Brian Farkas for not firing me when I told him I was writing a humorous book about religion. This book began as a Livejournal maintained between 2004 and 2006, and I cannot let the opportunity pass to thank the extraordinary collection of regular visitors—Catholic, Protestant, Orthodox, Anglican, Jewish, Sikh, Buddhist, Muslim, pagan, and atheist—who taught me so much and proved that the World Wide Web can indeed be a place for the fruitful exchange of ideas on contentious subjects like religion. Finally, I wish to thank my father and my brother, to whom this work is dedicated. Actual scholars and genuine Christians, I could ask for nothing greater than to follow in their footsteps.

INTRODUCTION

THE INTERNET THEOLOGIAN SPEAKS

Unless you have been marooned on a desert island or have spent the last several years in a cult that shuns electricity, you're almost certainly aware of me.

I am the Internet Theologian.

That is not my given name (which is Tom). It's the name thrust upon me by legions of awestruck admirers and by broken, embittered foes on the great ocean of ones and zeroes we call the Internet. I did not choose this *nom de data*, but I embrace it.

There is one thing in the world I love above all others: accuracy. Particularly, accuracy on the subject of Christianity. For years, I have patrolled the byways of the World Wide Web to correct errors, right wrongs, do battle with ignorance, and make fun of people with bad grammar.

I have done this not for glory or —heaven knows— monetary reward, but rather for the sheer exultation of serving Truth or, at the very least, Something Very Similar to Truth.

Although in my characteristically humble fashion, I preferred anonymity, it was not long before the lightning-bright nature of my insights and the obvious wealth of knowledge I possess soon led to hundreds of wisdom-hungry Web users beating a path to my e-door. Before long, I became a kind of guru figure, unanimously selected for the high honor of comoderator on a Livejournal community. It was then that I knew I had to take the next step in Internet Theology.

I had to become a Book Theologian.

The Internet is the single most important communications tool since the invention of CB radio. No one doubts the awesome power it wields in instantly disseminating crucial facts, information, and photographs of drunken celebrities all over the world. However, let's be honest: being famous on the Internet is a little like getting a Ph.D. by mail order. The only people likely to be impressed are other fake Ph.D.s and the hopelessly moronic.

So it was a desire to establish once and for all my theological credentials that led me to the bold fifteenth-century technology of the book—that plus a driving urge to show up obnoxious e-rivals such as "atheistdude" on Livejournal and "BibleGuy001" on Beliefnet.

However, if I was going to take the plunge and grace the medium of the printed page with my insights, I wasn't going to write some boring theological treatise heavy on words like "ontic" and "apophaticism" and "bibliography."

No, for my book, I would choose a subject both profound and gripping, something to excite the casual reader and flabbergast the jaded professor. Since the Internet—a venue for the flowering of popular culture as well as a tool for the mainstreaming of pornography—was the birthplace of my pedantry, it was only natural to turn to popular culture and its effect on Christianity as my grand subject.

"Wait a second," you are undoubtedly objecting. "Pop culture and Christianity? How can those two go together? I thought Christianity was supposed to be boring and life-less, the province of tenured snobs who couldn't craft a decent sentence if their faculty lounge depended on it. Whereas pop culture is actually quite fun."

Such sentiment shows that you have much to learn, O reader.

You may be surprised to learn this, but pop culture is how the vast majority of Americans express themselves religiously. A recent study shows that eight out of ten Americans say they worship God primarily through rock concerts, extreme sports, and T-shirts.[1] Today's Christians believe it's possible to be religious by shopping, watching TV, listening to their iPods, or applying fish bumper stickers to their cars.

That's because Americans largely think in terms of popular culture: simple messages attractively conveyed are the primary means by which we communicate with each other today.

Americans, in other words, have taken to Christianity the way we've taken to everything else—with an orgy of scatter-brained, well-meaning-but-crazy exertions that ultimately leave everyone feeling exhausted and slightly queasy. And when these exertions find a public expression, that expression is what Americans do better than anyone in the world:[2] pop culture.

As a result, today's Christianity is first and foremost dynamic. It is not merely something people are guilted

---

[1] Source: a recent study.
[2] Except the Japanese.

into doing on Sundays by their nagging, churchy spouses. While that may have been true for our boring parents and their irrelevant forms of worship, today the varieties of religious expression include not just church, but rock concerts, skateboarding competitions, wrestling matches, video games, bestselling novels, major motion pictures, and tiny comic books telling you the Devil invented trick-or-treating as a way to lure unsuspecting children into eternal damnation.

Of course, this vast exchange of ideas between Christianity and popular culture is not without critics. Aside from the egghead brigade, you have a number of Christians who wonder whether it's appropriate to produce a version of the Word of God billed as "The Get Funky Bible 4 Xtreme Teens."

While the professors can be dismissed as clueless killjoys, it behooves us to take the objections of concerned Christians seriously. Many Christian traditions—generally the smaller ones, like the Catholics and the Orthodox—argue that Christianity has to be correct in form as well as content. In other words, as it says in the Bible, "The medium is the message." Tinker too much with the way in which Christian truth is presented, these people argue, and you will alter the very nature of that truth.

Generally, such people can be forgiven because they are old. They have never thrilled to a well-delivered clown Mass, nor have they purchased any CDs by the top Christian death metal acts. Their antiquated notion of culture runs to composers like Mozart and Shakespeare and Dick Clark.

Despite valid criticisms of such people, this book takes their objections seriously as it wrestles with the question of whether it's theologically correct to promote Bible reading by putting new lyrics to the tune "Baby Got Back."

However, understanding pop culture is one thing—it's young, hip, and everywhere around us. But Christianity is something else altogether, a vast and complex subject, whose history spans nearly two thousand years and which has taken root in all corners of the globe. Surely, to understand a faith as multifaceted as Christianity, one needs a great deal of skill and expertise. One must be trained in navigating the treacherous territory between honest critique and grievous insult. One must possess a range of knowledge that is truly daunting: theology, culture, history, and the ways in which all these intersect.

Sure. That is, if one is a grade-grubbing Poindexter who's never kissed a girl in his life.

I'm referring here to the so-called experts who have monopolized public discussion of religion for decades: professors, theologians, scholars, pundits, bishops, saints, etc. These tiresome know-it-alls have a vested interest in making their subject matter seem imposing and difficult to master, requiring years of intensive, boring study of completely useless subjects like Greek.[3]

Here's a characteristic illustration of the sleep-inducing nonsense I'm talking about:

> For the word of God declares that the preaching 'although in itself true and most worthy of belief' is not sufficient to reach the human heart, unless a certain power be imparted to the speaker from God, and a grace appear upon his words; and it is only by the divine agency that this takes place in those who speak effectually.

I apologize to those few who have not dropped this book after immediately falling into a trance-like slumber.

---

[3] Yuck! (ὐυκ!)

The author of the above passage calls himself or herself "Origen."[4] I have no idea who that is, but I know who it *isn't*: a relevant author who knows how to make his subject sizzle.

You'd be amazed at how common this is. "Origen" is not the only offender. Everywhere you look, the study of religion is dressed up in fancy-pants rhetoric for the sole purpose of scaring off anyone who lacks the confidence to point to the obscurantists and say: "Hey! That emperor is buck naked!"

Let's presume, therefore, that any tweed-elbowed tenure monkeys who are reading this book are readying their quill pens in barely contained excitement at this moment.

Internet Theologian, they are preparing to say, *despite your obvious charm and youthful good looks, you have made a serious error in attempting a book on Christianity and pop culture. Christianity, you see, was never meant to mix with popular culture. On the contrary: the study of Christianity is such a dull, monotonous exercise that society is willing to pay us fabulous sums to devote our lives to writing seminar papers about it.*

If this were, in fact, the Internet, I would respond to this with an insouciant "LMAO" or an appropriately irreverent "smiley face" icon. You will have to use your imagination for that part.

However, since the conventions of the book form demand complete sentences and discourage excessive use of acronyms, I will instead respond thusly: Hogwash, Professor Doldrum. Religion and pop culture not only make a good pair — *they've been combined ever since the foundation of Christianity.*

As a matter of fact, I will go further: not only *can* we consider pop culture and Christianity together, but we

---

[4] P.S., genius: it's spelled "origin."

will be *unable* to understand contemporary Christianity without doing so.

[I will pause here until academia's ivory towers cease reverberating with the anguished screams of senior faculty.]

The reason those scholars are wailing is because they see their monopoly crumbling. Once people realize that they can understand Christianity by contemplating spoof rap videos on YouTube, those people will naturally ask, "Why waste months fighting your way through St. Augustine Hippo's *Civitas Dei* when you can listen to a vaguely punk-sounding song by a Christian group that says more or less the same thing? After all, isn't that the medium Hippo would be working in if he were alive today?"

St. Hippo, actually, presents us with an excellent illustration of the futility of trying to become an expert on religious matters through so-called "traditional" means.

As the story goes, the great saint was spending day and night trying to understand the Trinity, the description of God that lies at the heart of all Christian theology. How could something be three yet one? What were the precise relations between the Father, Son, and Holy Spirit? Was one created first, or were all three coeternal?

In other words, he was a real buzzkill. People stopped inviting him to parties. Other bishops referred to him as "St. Ponderous the Long-Winded." He even fell behind in writing sermons castigating the Donatists,[5] which was a real problem because, at the time, sermons castigating heretical sects were the closest thing people had to professional sports.

---

[5] An early heretical sect which argued that Christians who abjured the faith under torture should be forced to give up the choice parking spots at Christmas and Easter.

But then, in the midst of this boring and unproductive labor, the man known to his friends as "Augie" had a dream: he was walking along a beach and saw a young boy using a seashell to carry water from the ocean and dump it out on the sandy shore.

Chuckling at the futile labor of this youngster, Augustine walked over and asked, "So, tell me, do you think you'll be able to empty out the whole ocean?"

To which the boy replied, "Certainly — I'll be done before you manage to explain complex theological problems without using PowerPoint presentations and upbeat rock songs."

Upon waking, Augustine immediately began his masterwork: a three-minute rock song about the Trinity called "Jesus is the Gnarliest." This composition is still frequently performed today, which is more than I can say about *Civitas Dei*.

Fortunately, we moderns don't need to rely on precocious tots in dreams for our insights about religion, because we have the Internet. This amazing, all-embracing tool has broken theology and other fields wide open, simultaneously rendering universities and X-rated movie theaters alike obsolete. Our generation, unbound by the fetters of the past, no longer struggles beneath the unobtainable burden of a laminated library card. All we need is a cable connection and a computer costing in the neighborhood of a thousand dollars.

But don't expect the cabal of scholars to lead the way on this bold use of technology. No, a work based on the groundbreaking possibilities opened up by the Internet had to come from outside the ranks of the smug, egg-headed knowledge burglars ensconced in their ivory towers. It had to come from one well-versed in the only medium that combines the quality scholarship of an anonymous flyer with the dynamic community spirit of a "Lord of the Rings" convention.

It had to come from the Internet Theologian.

The burden is not light, friends; of that you can be sure. I have been obliged to make Google a virtual second home; I have become more familiar with Wikipedia than with my own extended family; I have tirelessly patrolled chatrooms, message boards, and newsgroups with the skill of a master jeweler searching a diamond for flaws. This work has taken literally *hours* over the course of the last six months.

I quickly realized what this undertaking did *not* require. I didn't need to go to graduate school to get some paper degree in useless, arcane subjects like "Church History" or "Sacred Theology" or "English." I didn't have to spend years of my life in a dusty seminar room wondering what Basil the Great could have possibly meant when he said, "I believe in God, but I don't believe God exists."[6] And, thank goodness, I didn't have to set foot in a single library. The Internet was my rod and my staff; it not only comforted me, it enabled me to stalk ex-girlfriends on MySpace while simultaneously doing research on the Council of Chalcedon.

While doing this very research, I came upon a striking truth. My subject matter is far from a new phenomenon, although I am arguably its definitive chronicler. With the help of the Internet, I have prepared the following chronology, tracing in rough form how through the centuries, the rich chocolate of Christianity has blended with the creamy peanut butter of popular culture to form an especially delicious Reese's cup of understanding.

---

[6] Answer: it was a pun.

CHRISTIANITY

A FAITH, A BROADWAY MUSICAL, AND A LONG-RUNNING DRAMEDY

45 A.D.: St. Paul, visiting Corinth, organizes the first ever Extreme Sports for Jesus Festival. Although the festival is well attended, it is ultimately considered a failure when three skateboarders are injured attempting a difficult stunt and the entire motocross contingent is sewn into snake-filled bags by Roman centurions.

90 A.D.: St. John the Divine writes *Revelation: The Apocalypse Factor*, which later loses its subtitle. Eventually chosen as the final book in the New Testament, marginal notations on a few surviving manuscript fragments indicate it was originally intended as an early installment in the James Bond franchise.

125 A.D.: Anticipating the practice of rappers by more than 1,800 years, a Christian apologist adopts the nom-de-groove "Justin Martyr" when explicating his "funky fresh" theological mix of Christianity and Platonism. The name turns out to be prophetic, though, and his career is cut short after only two albums.

248 A.D.: Centuries before the "blockbuster battles" between liberal and conservative authors shook up America's bookstores, Christian apologist Origen and pagan philosopher Celsus exchanged witty barbs in a series of bestselling treatises. Although only Origen's *Contra Celsum* survives, some early codices indicate that at least one other work was probably called "Celsus Is a Big Fat Idiot."

323 A.D.: To counter the growing popularity of Arianism, which is spread in part by attaching new lyrics to popular songs, the orthodox party produces *Triune!*, an all-singing, all-dancing musical extravaganza featuring blockbuster numbers like "Three Persons At Once" and "Dad, I'm Just Like You (Only Younger)." The production's success not only throws the Arian party into disarray, it makes its author, St. Athanasius, the most successful musical theater impresario of his era, his reputation surviving even lackluster affairs like *Exile Or Bust* and *Damn Heretics*.

368 A.D.: Sts. Basil, Gregory the Theologian, and Gregory of Nyssa form The Cappadocians, considered by scholars to be the world's first doo-wop group. Their hit, "I Believe in My Baby (But I Don't Believe My Baby Exists)," tops Byzantine charts for months. The group ends in discord, though, when Basil refuses to change his name to Gregory.

451 A.D.: The Council of Chalcedon concludes with the orthodox party proclaiming, in the words of the bishops present, "This is the faith of the Fathers and of the Apostles. Through Leo, Peter has spoken." The "Leo" referred to here is MC Leo T Great, first of the so-called "rhyme battle pontiffs," who dominated the fifth century with their incisive and electrifying hip-hop microphone skills. For centuries afterward, the non-Chalcedonian Christians are disparaged as "sucker MCs."

529 A.D.: Benedict of Nursia establishes the monastery of Monte Cassino, the first such order in Western Europe. What is less known is that Monte Cassino was also arguably the world's first comedy club and that St. Benedict is the father not only of Western monasticism, but also the two-drink minimum and "Laff-a-Lot Fridays," where couples get in for half price.

754 **A.D.:** The first Council of Constantinople settles the question of iconoclasm with a steel cage match. *For now.*

787 **A.D.:** A capacity crowd is on-hand as the orthodox party reclaims the World Heavyweight Championship, triumphs in a "Hell in a Cell" match, and settles the question of iconoclasm once and for all, thanks to a surprise run-in during the match by Pope Adrian I.

1054 **A.D.:** The Great Schism between Eastern and Western Christianity is sealed, not by mutual excommunications between pope and patriarch, but following a ferocious dance-off that pits the papal ambassador to Constantinople against the funkiest body-poppers in the Byzantine Empire.

1095 **A.D.:** Pope Urban II, one of the most successful moguls of his day, has the hit of his career with *Crusade*. So popular is this that a number of sequels are rushed into production, each one slightly less inspired than the one before. By the time of *Crusade IV: Fratricide*, critics and audiences agree that the franchise is creatively bankrupt.

1202 **A.D.:** St. Francis of Assisi invents Christian hippies. It will take the invention of the acoustic guitar, though, to bring this innovation to its full, most annoying fruition.

1309–1377 **A.D.:** *The Babylonian Captivity,* a long-running sketch comedy series by the improv troupe known as the Avignon Popes, is the talk of Europe.

1517 **A.D.:** The Protestant Reformation succeeds where previous reform movements failed, thanks to the invention of a key piece of communication technology that is still with us today: graffiti. Martin Luther's huge spray-painted mural on the door of the Wittenberg Castle Church—a work known as the "Ninety-five Pieces" for the number of separate design elements—sets off the intellectual and political ferment of the Reformation.

1545–1563 **A.D.:** *Reformation 2: The Papacy Strikes Back* (or, as it was known upon its American release, *Counter-Reformation*) opens across Europe to mixed reviews. In general, it is a hit with Catholic audiences, but Protestant crowds largely stay home. As critic Martin Luther panned, "I am more afraid of my own heart than of the pope and all his cardinals. I have within me the great pope, Self."[7] He also called it "predictable and overwrought" and said the love interest "feels tacked on."

1600 **A.D.:** St. Francis de Sales wins a huge number of French Protestants to Catholicism through a strongly negative direct mail campaign, that portrays the Reformers as out of touch, corrupt, and soft on crime. The memorable tagline of one piece of mail runs, "John Calvin—How Can We Trust Him with Our

---

[7] This is a genuine quote actually spoken by Martin Luther. Google it! I think you'll be pleasantly surprised!

Salvation When We Can't Even Trust Him to Clean Up Geneva?"

1649–1660 A.D.: A period of tremendous religious ferment in England follows the execution of King Charles "the First" Stuart and the establishment of a republic. The various religious groups express themselves in countless thousands of cheaply printed pamphlets, making them the seventeenth-century's version of bloggers. Unlike today's spineless leaders, though, Oliver Cromwell has the common sense to throw them in prison.

1750 A.D.: Deism—the belief that God exists but does not intervene in his creation—becomes fashionable among intellectuals in Europe and America. The movement is promoted by a hilarious, long-running newspaper comic strip called *The Adventures of Johnny Seeker and the Great Watchmaker.*

1780s A.D.: The Wesley Brothers enjoy a string of Top Ten singles in Britain that will go unbroken for nearly 200 years, until the Beatles top charts with their own smash versions of "I Want to Hold Your Hand," "Hard Day's Night," and "Come, Thou Long-expected Jesus."

1828 A.D.: The long-anticipated sequel to the blockbuster the *Great Awakening* arrives in the form of the *Second Great Awakening: Escape from the Burned-over District.* Although ticket sales are strong, many reviewers argue that this installment lacks the character development and nuance of the original.

1844 A.D.: William Miller, preacher and producer of several spectacularly successful Christian dramas, announces a show for fall that he promises will be "the program to end all programs." In the end, Miller's new series is so underwhelming that wags dub it the "Great Disappointment." Though swiftly canceled, it regularly appears in reruns even to this day.

1925 A.D.: "You'll Never Make a Monkey out of Me" becomes the most popular song in the nation after being performed in the Broadway smash *Scopes Trial Follies* by the two most prolific showmen of their era, the team known as Darrow & Bryant.

1963 A.D.: Pope John XXIII begins the Second Vatican Council by quoting the entirety of Bob Dylan's "Blowin' In the Wind." Papal biographers will later claim that His Holiness originally intended to open with Little Richard's "Tutti Frutti," but this is never established beyond doubt.

2007 A.D.: Thanks to the magic of digital editing, St. Justin Martyr duets with slain rapper Tupac Shakur on the hit, "All Eyez On Tha Logos."

So you see, Christianity and pop culture have been linked for millennia, with Christians often using cultural forms to explain their faith.

In the United States, this trend is even more pronounced. In fact, exploring Christianity through pop culture may even be characteristic of Americans, as earlier media were for earlier Christians—as philosophy was for the Greeks, for example, or as bloody civil war was for the Germans.

The first book printed in the American colonies, after all, was the famous *Bay Psalm Book*—a religious book designed to get groups of people singing, which was both a good way to stop thinking about witchcraft and starvation and the only form of recreation that didn't incur a flogging sentence from Puritan magistrates.

So it has followed, with many other pop culture "firsts" racked up by Christians in America. Joseph Smith: inventor of the game "Scattegories." Cyrus Schofield: Bible publisher and the first man to play rhythm guitar in a heavy metal band. Aimee Semple McPherson: creator of "Soul Train." From movies to music to tag team wrestling, if you look closely enough, you'll find Christianity.

And why should it be otherwise? Look at Jesus himself. He spoke in parables, which were considered the reality TV of their day. Granted, that sounds horrendously boring to you and me, but remember: Jesus lived literally decades before the invention of TiVo. People in first century Galilee were lucky to hear a good parable now and then; it broke up the tedium of succumbing to heat stroke while forking over all your possessions to the figurehead monarch installed by Rome. They positively lined up for a top parable-sayer; in fact, my research suggests there were probably ticket scalpers at the Sermon on the Mount.

But you're not likely to get any of this valuable information in dull university classes or unreadable textbooks. Why? Because so-called scholars frown on the methods of research employed by the Internet Theologian—namely, skimming the results of Google searches and filling in the blanks with speculation.

Yes, my methodology is bold and unconventional, and not everyone will be fully prepared for the kind of no-holds-barred learning experience this book provides. So I offer the following advice.

First, there will be times in the course of this book when you will scratch your head and say, "I never knew that before. I'd better double-check it." However, your fact-checking efforts will come to naught, because many of the statements I use to make points in this book are "pre-facts": that is, they are statements that sound plausible, but for which there is as yet no *conclusive* evidence to establish their accuracy.

Naturally, some people will object to this methodology.[8] However, this is perfectly consistent with long-established scientific and scholarly practice. After all, if Galileo of Galilee had waited for "scholars" and "facts" to catch up with him, he might never have proved that the sun moves backwards at night.

In addition to the pre-fact, I have relied upon another means of conveying truth that may prove controversial to the sort of person who has not kissed a girl since Dukakis was president. This is the method of research that I call "nontraditional sourcing."

In "traditional" (read: boring) circles, it's generally accepted that there are only a few valid ways of getting information: from "primary sources," like incredibly dull documents that no one cares about or by talking to old people about the Great Depression; or from "secondary sources," which are—if you can believe this—books *about* those dull documents and old people. In other words, your sources are either coming from scholars, or from the

---

[8] You know who you are, "professor."

dense, pricey books they churn out on a regular basis to dominate the public discussion. Sounds like a pretty good racket, doesn't it? It's things like this that make it clear why the U.S. Attorney General has referred to scholars as "the most vicious criminal syndicate in America."[9]

Since the Internet Theologian is not a provincial, narrow-minded yokel, I believe other forms of sourcing should be included in important works like this one. For example: most scholars would not consider, say, a scrap of conversation I overheard in an elevator as a "reliable" source of information about the Bible. Yet is this "way of knowing" any less valid than the narrow, Western method?

Taking the methodology of compiling sources normally found on the Internet as my inspiration, I have relied on a range of nontraditional ways of uncovering crucial knowledge: rumors, things I kind of remember hearing at parties, statements from anonymous pamphlets written in all capital letters, stuff my friend Marc[10] tells me, and — most importantly — *things that I believe should be true.* If there's one thing you can learn from the Internet, it's that you should never let "the facts" stand in the way of what you believe in, whether that's the One True Faith or your choice for best episode ever of *Buffy the Vampire Slayer.*[11]

The reader should not assume, though, that because I am unafraid to rely upon the formidable powers of my own subconscious in assembling this book that it is entirely free of what professional academics still insist upon calling "accurate information."

Indeed, the scholarliness of this work can be deduced

---

[9] This is an example of a "pre-fact."

[10] He has a Web site!

[11] Episode #5V19, "I Only Have Eyes For You" (first run date: April 28, 1998).

by simply directing your attention to the bottom of the page, to find in abundance those telltale marks of scholarship that are characteristic of the Serious Work: footnotes.[12]

Don't assume that just anyone can write a book with footnotes. The U.S. Department of Scholarliness has stringent guidelines about exactly which works are eligible for footnote funding, and only a certain number of books per year are so favored.[13]

In summary, what you hold in your hands is an impassioned attempt to explain, for the confused and bewildered, the places where religion intersects with popular culture and what this means for Christianity, America, and the future of movies marketed to audiences who don't think there should be any swearing in war films.

This work is not only cutting edge, entertaining, and life-changing, it's also downright necessary. Religion is at the forefront of public debate in America in a way it hasn't been since the great Civil Rights Era, when the Rev. Martin "Junior" Luther issued the famous Emancipation Proclamation from the steps of Faneuil Hall, with its immortal opening phrase: "Fourscore and seven years ago, I come not to praise Caesar, but to bury him."

A great deal of the debate around the role of religion in public life, though, stems from ignorance about what religion really is. Despite America's reputation as a country in which a majority of citizens are Christian, many Americans cannot explain some of the very basic elements of the Christian faith, such as Jesus' precise relationship to his Father, and who the guy wearing the funny hat

---

[12] Like this one!

[13] This is an example of a "pre-fact."

is.[14] In fact, a national survey found that only three in ten Americans can correctly identify Jesus as one of the Persons of the Holy Trinity, while a disheartening 40 percent of our fellow citizens think Jesus was a backup singer for Santana in the 1970s.[15]

With such irrefutable empirical evidence at our disposal, it's impossible to say that ignorance of Christianity is limited to non-Christians. Indeed, this ignorance is a widespread problem, affecting all levels of society to the point where a solid plurality of Catholic priests now express the belief that the Bible regards baptism as "a warm-weather sacrament."

Clearly, such a situation calls for immediate correction. But the great stumbling block preventing many of us from learning about religion is that, let's face it: religion is often extremely boring. That's why, as God wrote in his bestselling book, *Bible*, we're called upon to "zest it up a little."[16]

Here the Internet Theologian comes to your rescue.

The truth—artfully concealed by those aforementioned eggheads—is, you don't need a pile of dull books with titles like *Acta Sanctorum* and *Institutes of Christian Religion* and *Finnegan's Wake* to understand Christianity.

My dear readers, the only book you need is this one.

---

[14] He's the pope.

[15] Source: a national survey.

[16] I don't have the precise citation in front of me, but I'm sure it's in there. Maybe in the Book of Gandalf.

HOLD YOUR FIRE
A NOTE TO THE INTEMPERATE

It is not lost on the Internet Theologian that in our day and age, religion is an extremely sensitive subject. Many religious people are quite adamant that their faith should not be mocked, derided, or, frankly, discussed by outsiders.

This work is not intended to insult or offend anyone,[17] but it's worth saying at the outset that any work dealing with religion in an on-the-edge format such as this will ruffle a few feathers. Hopefully not the kind of feathers that get together to set fire to embassies, but even in that case, my attitude is—can only be—"let it come."

In the era of the Internet Theologian, one must be fearless. One must not shirk from the courage of one's convictions because, as St. Paul memorably asked, "What the hell good did shirking ever do anybody?" We cannot allow concerns about offensiveness, taste, or accuracy to get in the way of bold and inventive explorations of faith and its changing nature.

I, for one, will not be cowed. To any who see in this work anything other than a courageous voyage to the heart of a great faith and its connection with a great way to sell DVDs, I say: Pour forth your scorn. I do not fear it. You will not intimidate me into backing away from my convictions.

If this work causes offense, let the chips fall where they may. Inquiries like this one have a long tradition of flying in the face of popular opinion. I link my endeavor to those of Socrates, Galilee Galilestro, Scopes T. Monkeytrial, and the people who looked into whether the voting on *American Idol* is rigged. Our lot may be a lonely one,

---

[17] Except scholars.

but it is a noble calling: to go forth into the dark caverns of human ignorance bearing the blazing beacons of pre-facts and nontraditional sourcing, and letting all who will behold the truth, behold it.

I repeat: I am not afraid of giving offense.

If, however, you are deeply offended and seeking to address your complaints to someone, I suggest you use this handy, pre-addressed form:

I promise I will swiftly answer each and every complaint or—at the very least—glance quickly at the postcard before putting it down somewhere and forgetting about it.[18]

And with that, we begin our journey to explore once and for all how it is that Americans use pop culture to understand Christianity. We go boldly, and without fear of giving offense![19]

---

[18] Are you sure you really want to cut this out? It will leave a big hole in your book . . .

[19] But remember the handy form just in case you are offended.

EVERYTHING YOU NEED TO KNOW ABOUT CHRISTIANITY

MINUS THE BORING PARTS

America in the twenty-first century is a land divided. We are not only divided by the old causes — race, geography, use of the term "pop" versus the term "soda" — but even by what theoretically should be a source of unity: hatred of the New York Yankees.

Sharper still than that great conflict, though, is the saddening battle fought over religion. The increasingly acrid dispute over faith now colors everything — politics, culture, sports, even children's cartoon shows.[1] Indeed, there are many knowledgeable observers of the American scene who predict that the next great conflict to define our society will be not between Republicans and Democrats or conservatives and liberals, but between people who have Christian fish bumper stickers and those who have similar bumper stickers, but with feet appended to the fish.

---

[1] See, for instance, the recent cable series, *The Adventures of Billy Secular and His Theocracy-Busters.*

Yes, this great struggle pits ardent religious believers — particularly the sort of Christians who go to church on Wednesday nights — against equally vehement foes of all religions.

This is especially sad because it's so familiar in American history. You would think we would learn from our mistakes, but with our young people spending the bulk of their history classes text-messaging each other about the most violent rap groups around, it seems we are doomed to repeat the past since we cannot learn from it, just as Obi-Wan Kenobi foretold.

The earliest European settlers of America were, of course, motivated largely by a completely whacked-out version of Christianity and were extraordinarily uninterested in hearing polite disagreement about it. This history of intolerance is personified by Massachusetts woman Anne Hutchinson, who was banished from her native colony to Rhode Island and then turned out to be so annoying that not even laid-back colonial hippie Roger Williams could put up with her.

Not to put too fine a point on it, but having Roger Williams boot you out of Rhode Island for your divergent religious beliefs is a little like having Wavy Gravy tell you he's worried about how much grass you're smoking.

At any rate, although Anne Hutchinson herself is quite spectacularly dead, her spirit lives on in the acidic debates between religious believers and secular unbelievers in America.

The Internet is, of course, a battlefront fraught with such conflict. There — in those sacred cyberhalls — the intensifying discord of our fractured civic life has made itself felt. And shockingly, but undeniably, information of a less-than-fully-accurate nature is being disseminated in

Internet arguments about religion.

This is particularly true along the faultline between the most savagely divided Internet partisans: fans of World of Warcraft versus fans of Everquest.

A slightly less ferocious (but equally notable) online struggle is taking place between Christians and atheists, which is ironic, when you consider how similar their most annoying representatives are in tone and demeanor.

Listening to Christian Americans gripe about atheists and then listening to atheists complain about Christians is truly an exercise in "de ja vu all over again." Both groups make remarkably similar arguments: they're marginalized by the growing power of the other side; they feel as if their deeply held beliefs are held up for ridicule in the public square; they worry about the dangerous influence their antagonists have on policymakers; they cannot believe it's the twenty-first century and we're still stuck with the damn designated hitter rule.

But when pressed to describe exactly what is their *betes noires*,[2] most Americans are at a loss. Atheists, agnostics, and Democrats, for example, are quick to accuse Christians[3] of believing that just about everyone is going to burn eternally in a deeply unpleasant place called "Hell." What they don't realize is that there's no agreement among Christians about what Hell is, and that some of the smaller Christian denominations—such as

---

[2] A fancy French term whose meaning I am unclear about.

[3] And generally, when we talk about a conflict between religious believers and unbelievers in America, we're talking about Christians. For some reason, secular Americans just don't seem interested in going after Jews, Muslims, or Zoroastrians. Or even Buddhists! Come on—Buddhists aren't even going to fight back! Take a swing!

Catholics and the Orthodox—have had prominent theologians suggest that no one ever eternally goes to Hell.

By the same token, when Christians jeer that atheists, agnostics, and NPR listeners envision a bleak and absurd world devoid of meaning or purpose because of the lack of an afterlife, what they don't realize is that most unbelievers are patiently expecting the return of the Great Spacecraft, which will encase their brains in metal cylinders and whisk them away to the Planet Atheistica, where they will live forever.[4]

So you see, the gap isn't as wide as most believe. Christians are not all plotting to establish a *Handmaid's Tale*-esque theocracy in which not even Hollywood starlets can get divorced. And atheists, for their part, mostly don't sympathize with Hitler.

Healing this illusory rift requires nothing more complicated than a simple explanation of common terms, concepts, and groups—a "crib sheet," if you will, to the more esoteric aspects of faith in America. And who better qualified to provide this service than I? Why, I have spent literally *hours* skimming Wikipedia entries and chat room conversations, to the point where my grasp of Christianity, both sweeping and discerning, rivals that of such noted theologians as John Chrysostom and Gandalf.

Naturally, some will object, claiming that no one can possibly absorb the abundance of knowledge needed to properly understand Christianity in the span of a few hundred words. An appropriate grasp of such learning can be acquired only after years of patient and persistent study of

[4] Source: a cult's Internet site, poorly translated from the Korean.

long, dull theology tomes written by authors with unpronounceable German names, these people argue.

These people are called "losers." And these losers are mistaken, because everything you need to know about Christianity—and, in fact, more—is contained in these pages.

And, let's face it, it's not like you're ever going to need to know all this stuff in great detail. All you really need is a way to silence antagonists on Internet message boards and wow impressionable dolts at cocktail parties. Just say a bunch of words like "*abecedarian*" and "Council of Chalcedon," and adversaries will be suitably awed and subdued by your prowess. Not only that, but their utter unwillingness to challenge your demonstrable authority will allow you to move away from these unnecessary arguments and focus instead on what the Internet is really good for: hilarious viral videos and MP3 downloads of questionable legality.

And if not, well, maybe you're going to the wrong cocktail parties.

I provide the following, therefore, not in the sterile, apolitical service of knowledge, but as a means to bind up our nation's wounds, to get past the half-truths and lies that divide us, so that we may join together as one and focus on combating the enemies who truly menace us from without.

I'm referring, of course, to the New York Yankees and their hateful fans.

A USEFUL GUIDE
for Atheists, Agnostics, Democrats, and Clueless Christians

> *Section 1—Major Christian Groups and How to Spot Them on the Subway*

Uninformed Americans tend to lump all Christians together—broad distinctions like Catholic and Protestant are lost on them, to say nothing of fine distinctions like Arminians vs. Preterists, Monothelites vs. Monophysites, or stalactites vs. stalagmites.[5] This section, an exhaustive survey of all Christian denominations, splinters, factions, and major singing groups, should provide a helpful introduction to an oft-confusing world.

Catholics: Catholics are the Boston Celtics of Christianity. They have one of the oldest and most successful franchises (despite a recent drought in terms of winning championships) and continue to pack in the fans year after year. When people think of "the Church," they generally think of the Catholic Church: stern prelates denouncing errant politicians, black-clad priests chanting Latin in huge stone cathedrals, incense, candles, effigies of weeping saints. Of course, it's been years since any of that applied to the Catholics, and you're more likely to hear "Bringing in the Sheaves" at a Mass than "*Dies Irae*," but old habits die hard. Some things remain true, though, and Catholics still are not allowed to read the Bible, and they continue to believe the pope is magic. "Pope," when translated from Catholic to English, means "President."

---

[5] Stalagmites are the ones on the ground.

Protestants: Confusingly, the first Protestants were actually Catholics who disagreed with some of the pope's fundraising tactics. The sixteenth century being what it was, this minor quibble eventually developed into a series of bloody wars that engulfed all of Europe. Unlike the Catholics, though, who have to take orders from the magic pope, Protestants are pretty much free to do as they please, which is why there are more than thirty thousand separate Protestant denominations. Because listing all of them is basically an exercise in judicious placement of the words "Reformed," "Independent," and "First," it's better to simply look at the two major divisions within Protestantism:

Mainline Protestants: These are the folks famously summed up by Walt Whitman as "uptight white people at prayer."[6] They include, but are not limited to, various Lutherans, Congregationalists, Episcopalians, some Methodists, and the Arizona Cardinals. Although they were once among the most fiery and fulsome advocates of their own particular brands of Christianity, most mainline churches are now organized around the principle of not making a fuss.

Evangelical Protestants: These are the Protestants who strike fear in the hearts of atheists, liberals, mainline Protestants, and those Hollywood studios hoping to market films to "the heartland" successfully. Most Southern Baptists are evangelical, as are some Presbyterians,

---

[6] Source: a thing I wish Walt Whitman would have said.

Methodists, and virtually all major league pitchers who thank Jesus for their breaking ball. To outsiders, evangelical Protestants are the shock troops of a new theocracy, when in reality what most of them want to do is record a really super new pop-country song about the Bible. Nonbelievers often lazily link evangelical Protestants with Catholics in terms of their political import, which is ironic since evangelicals criticize Catholics for never reading the Bible and worshipping Mary while Catholics in turn denounce evangelicals for completely screwing up every attempt to cook a decent Italian meal.

Orthodox Christians: Until recently, most scholars agreed that Orthodox Christians didn't exist. Like werewolves, fairies, and Romanians, they were simply a charming Old World fable designed to delight children with outlandish details regarding rich, luxurious beards and interminable arguments about the proper interpretation of Greek words. Upon further reflection, some scholars now cautiously hazard the guess that there are roughly 250 million Orthodox Christians in the world, with a lineage stretching back to the earliest days of the Church. As for what these strange, chanting, hirsute folk actually believe, though, no one is yet confident enough to hazard a guess.

Pentecostals: These are Christians who, angered by the lack of shouting and gesticulating in mainline Protestant faiths, went ahead and started their own movement at a Los Angeles church possibly called ZuZu's Petals.[7] Although not the only Christian movement to have started in America (indeed, if Christian movements were gold bullion, America would have no national debt), Pentecostalism may well be the most important. It is the fastest-growing Christian movement in the world and, as its beliefs evolve (in some cases into forms radically different from historically orthodox Christianity), many scholars suggest it should be considered a fourth major branch of the Christian tradition, along with Catholicism, Orthodoxy, and Protestantism. Which makes it even weirder that no one you know goes to a Pentecostal church.

Mormons: This is a somewhat controversial selection, because a great many Christians—particularly evangelical Protestants—insist that Mormons, or "Saturday Saints" as they prefer to be called, aren't really Christians at all. To Catholics and Orthodox Christians, this "Katie bar the door" approach is somewhat questionable, considering how many weirdo Protestant groups there are. Nonetheless, Mormons are here, they're not going away, and their relentless expansion, fueled by a desire to both stamp out caffeine and win an NBA championship for the perennially underachieving Utah Jazz, cannot be stopped. So, while we wait for the first Mormon president to shutter our jittery nation's espresso bars, it's worth taking a second to look at some common myths and stereotypes about Mormons.

---

[7] It was something like that, right? Help me out here. I'm having no luck on my various wiki sites.

> Statement: Mormons do not drink alcohol or use tobacco. (True)
> Statement: Mormons are made of sugar and melt when it rains. (False)
> Statement: In addition to the Bible, Mormons revere a third holy book called the Book of Mormon. (True)
> Statement: Mormons have telepathic powers and can read your thoughts. (True)

Unitarians: They're not really Christians at this point, but I can't resist pointing out a hilarious claim by supposed genius Thomas Jefferson: "I rejoice that in this blessed country of free inquiry and belief, which has surrendered its conscience to neither kings or priests, the genuine doctrine of only one God is reviving, and I trust that there is not a young man now living in the United States who will not die a Unitarian."[8] Ha! Good call, Mr. Inventor-of-the-Dumbwaiter. Boy, apparently you could design Monticello, but you couldn't *count*! Seriously, nothing against the Unitarians, but could Jefferson have been more wrong? What a schmuck!

Section 2—The Bible: Don't Worry; You Don't Have to Read the Whole Thing

For most Christian groups that don't revolve around the scrawled prophecies of armed lunatics, the Bible is the

---

[8] I came across Jefferson's hilariously wrong-footed prediction in Stephen Prothero's excellent American Jesus. Readers should be warned, thought, that the Prothero book is an actual work of scholarship by an actual scholar, and therefore contains far fewer uses of the word "schmuck" than the present volume.

text of central importance. Critics of Christianity, though, commonly assume that all Christians are in agreement on the Bible and what it means, when nothing could be farther from the truth. In fact, Christians have been arguing about the Bible since before it existed, which is kind of a paradox. This section surveys the major views on biblical interpretation among Christians.

Authorship: Most Christians believe that the individual books of the Bible were written by the authors they're named for; thus, Christians believe the Lamentations of Jeremiah were written by Jeremiah, that the Gospel According to John was written by John, that the Book of Numbers was written by Joey Numbers, etc. Most scholars, by contrast, argue that most books in the Bible couldn't have been written by the people they're attributed to. Instead, using the sort of precision analysis and painstaking research for which they're paid top dollar, these scholars conclude that the books of the Bible must have been written by . . . someone. (It's declarations like this one that have convinced our society to stop paying attention to scholars, and we're all the better for it.)

Canonicity: This is a fancy word for "popularity contest." This is how the various Greek bishops of the fourth century decided which books should be in the Bible and which should hereafter be banished to volumes with titles like "The Oxford Compendium of Miscellaneous Early Christian Writings." Basically, they had three criteria:[9] (1) Was this written by a big shot famous apostle? (2) Is this the kind of thing the

---

[9] Or, to use the original Greek, "criterions."

Gnostics will be able to twist easily to support their nonsense? (3) Would this make a good film? Potentially starring Harrison Ford as Paul?

As a result, suck-up apostles like Titus got their epistles included, while perfectly deserving early Christians like Frank "Shepherd" Hermas and Ted "Fragments" Papias were banished to the limbo of the "miscellaneous" compendium.

Interpretation: A sharp dividing line separates Protestants from other Christian groups on the question of interpretation. Protestants, particularly evangelical (or, in scholarly terminology, "Southern") Protestants, have historically argued that the Bible must be interpreted *literally*—that is, when John the Divine says, "Look out for that dragon!" *he means a dragon, damn it.* Atheists have historically had a field day with this position, pointing out, for example, that there are two separate and differing accounts of Creation in the Book of Genesis; that the New Testament gives two vastly different explanations for how Judas died; and that there certainly seem to be a lot of dragons toward the back of the book.

Some of the smaller denominations, like Catholics and the Orthodox, though, argue that literal interpretation is only part of how the Bible should be read. Origen, perhaps the greatest of early biblical exegetes,[10] argued that the Bible must be read in three ways: (1) literally, (2) allegorically, and (3) while jogging on a treadmill. (In addition to being an exegete, Origen was also a tremendous fitness buff.)

---

[10] This is a word professors use when they mean "explainer person."

Armed with Origen's approach, the smaller denominations have been historically untroubled by the sorts of arguments that can trip up unwary Protestants and, what's more, they generally have better cardio.

A̲u̲t̲h̲o̲r̲i̲t̲y̲: This is perhaps the most important point of contention on the subject of the Bible. The Protestant Reformation was characterized by two distinct battle cries: "*Sola scriptura!*[11]" and "Indulge *this*, Pope Monkeykisser!"[12] Protestants argued that Christians didn't need a clerical caste to interpret the Bible—particularly not the sort of corpulent, ruddy clerics eating fish with their hands like you see in Renaissance paintings. All Christians needed, argued the Protestants, was literacy, and by reading the text they would all reach the same conclusions about faith and God.

The centuries have passed and we've all had a pretty good laugh at this startling naïveté. Boy, the egg's really on Swingli's face, isn't it? Still, the Protestants have a good thing going, and insist on sticking with the whole "Scripture alone" deal. Catholics, meanwhile, aren't permitted to read the Bible. Only the Magic Pope is allowed to, and he parcels out what he learns with a certain terseness. Last Christmas, for example, he told anxious and curious Catholics at a Mass at St. Peter's Basilica, "There's a lot about sheep and shepherds in there. Frankly, I'm having a hard time following the narrative. I've been distracted, particularly with Notre Dame in a bowl game again. I'll pick it up after the holidays."

---

[11] Literally, "alone book." (Huh?)
[12] The early Reformers could be extraordinarily juvenile.

Section 3—The Afterlife: How to Book the Choicest Accommodations

Christianity, like other religions, seeks to answer the really compelling questions in life, such as, "How come nothing's open on Easter Sunday? Not even Subway, for crying out loud." Other important questions include: What happens when we die? Does our consciousness simply blink out of existence, as depressed undergraduates reading Camus for the first time insist; or does an immortal soul live on after we die? And if so, does the soul have pockets? Because I feel like it would be good to have somewhere to keep loose change. You never know when it's going to come in handy.

Heaven: Thanks to the illiterate yokels of the Middle Ages, our concepts about the afterlife have become permanently confused with the metaphorical descriptions of them that medieval preachers found handy when addressing audiences that thought flatulence was demonic.[13] So, when you hear the word "Heaven," you probably think of fluffy clouds and people dressed in white and playing harps for some reason.

In fact, most Christian groups are pretty quiet on what Heaven (or heaven, as the hip, new capitalization has it) will be like, except that God will be there,

---

[13] On the subject of demonic flatulence and other troubles of the Middle Ages, I cannot recommend strongly enough Norman Cohn's indispensable *Europe's Inner Demons*. This book will repay many repeated readings; however, like most such works of "traditional scholarship," it cannot match the present work in terms of "zingers."

and Mary, and the saints, and possibly the members of your family who died before you (though, let's be honest, probably not your Uncle Al). And that it will be awesome — *unimaginably* awesome.

In its most basic form, this term refers to the ultimate destiny of a certain number of souls. Depending on whom you listen to, heaven could be either: where all of us will end up (Origen); where many of us will end up (St. Gregory of Nyssa); where some of us will end up (John Calvin); where a small portion of us have, in some sense, already ended up (John of Leyden); where precisely 144,000 of us will end up (Charles Taze Russell); or where Jack Chick will end up (Jack Chick). Theologian Belinda Carlisle once posited that "Ooh, baby, heaven is a place on earth," but explorers combing the globe have yet to confirm this.

"Saints," incidentally, while generally portrayed as the superheroes of Christianity, are actually just those people whom church officials (Catholic or Orthodox or the occasional incense-loving Protestant) have decided are definitely in Heaven. Plus, the list of saints is not meant to be exhaustive — there are countless other people in Heaven; the church just doesn't know about them yet. Maybe even someone you knew (although, based on some of the people you know, I wouldn't expect to run into too many familiar faces beyond the Gates of Paradise).

Hell: Again, because of our slack-jawed, book-fearing foremorons, we're stuck with an image of Hell as a definite geographic location full of fire and ironic tortures (e.g., Fatty has to eat a lot, that person who insists on taking two parking spaces with their damned sports car has to watch it get keyed by teenagers, etc.). But not all Christian groups believe that Hell is a place of capering demons with pitchforks, or even a Dante-esque fantasia of concentric circles and former popes up to their necks in ordure. In fact, official Christian doctrine is relatively free of speculation about Hell. To wit:

The Catholic Church, while definitively proclaiming that some people (the New Orleans Saints) are in Heaven, has never said that anyone is definitely in Hell. Not even Judas. Boy, wouldn't it be weird to go to Heaven and run into Judas? "Man, they let anybody in here!" you would joke. He would smile and nervously shake his head (he doesn't speak English, you twit).

Protestants are generally split on Hell,[14] with some adopting a line similar to the Catholic approach (i.e., we don't know who's in Hell), while others, like the Puritans and their intellectual descendants, prefer to opine that, whoever's in Hell now, *you're* going there pretty soon, and they're kind of okay with that.

Some theologians from the Catholic, Protestant, and Orthodox camps now advance the idea that Hell, rather than being a literal place, is better thought of as a *condition*: not of eternal, ironic torment, but of never-ending separation from God, a kind of radical, terrible loneliness. While this makes some sense, it would also have made the first part of the *Divine Comedy* extraordinarily dull.

---

[14] Of course, Protestants are generally split on breakfast, so no surprise here.

Purgatory: Hey! Now *there's* a Rorschach test of a word for you. If you read the word "Purgatory" and thought, "Hmm, interesting, I'll read on," you're either a Catholic or a nonbeliever. If, however, your first reaction was to tear up this book and fulminate against the lies of the pope, you might be a Protestant.[15] If you sort of chuckled smugly to yourself, you're either an atheist or an Orthodox Christian.

That's because there are few doctrines more controversial than Purgatory, the Terrell Owens of afterlife options. Protestants reject it as unbiblical, Orthodox Christians say it's a case of the Catholics missing the forest for the trees, and Catholics threaten to bring back the Inquisition if everybody doesn't shut up.

Basically, Catholics and Orthodox Christians agree that there's some intermediate stage between Earth and Heaven. What that stage entails (a fruit cup? an in-flight magazine? encounter with a purifying spiritual fire?) is a source of contention. Protestants, though, are happy to stick with the either-or of Heaven and Hell.

Salvation: This is the basic question when it comes to the afterlife: Who gets a window seat on the Awesome Train, and who's stuck walking in the pouring rain all the way out to Upper East Hell? Well, that's how St. John of the Cross formulated it, anyway.[16]

The Bible itself offers mixed signals on this.

---

[15] You might even be Oliver Cromwell. Greetings, your Lord Protectorship!

[16] Source: It's totally out there in cyberspace. You're just googling it wrong.

Sometimes, it seems like Jesus is saying that God expects everyone to be saved, while other times it seems pretty clear that at least some people are in for an eternity of deep unpleasantness. Some of the major views are:

Apokatastasis: This extremely long Greek word (meaning, literally, "Dukakis-like furlough program") basically means "everyone gets off scot-free." It's sort of like what would happen if God were a Democrat. Origen, Gregory of Nyssa, and the awesomely-named Gregory Thaumaturge are the key early proponents of this theory. However, it fell into disfavor when Origen (or, possibly, just his backup singers, known as the Origen-ettes) suggested that even the Devil would be saved. Running into him in Heaven would be even more surprising than meeting Judas there, and marginally more of a shock than bumping into your Uncle Al.

Predestination: This was the doctrine, formulated by St. Augustine (known in his pro-wrestling days as "The Hippo") on an off-day, that God has already decreed that some people will go to Heaven and some will go to Hell. To the former, he sends help to keep them on the straight and narrow, while to the latter, he sends bees to sting and expensive transmission problems to vex. Surprisingly, this was so popular that John Calvin eventually rolled out a new model, called Double Deluxe Predestination, which promised twice the reprobation and twice the election at half the cost. Despite that, it has been remarkably unsuccessful with contemporary audiences.

anifest Destiny: Not really. I was just checking to see if you were paying attention. Lord knows I used to begin daydreaming in school as soon as the teacher started talking about predestination. Apparently, the Puritans thought it was the bee's knees. What a fun bunch they were, huh?

Section 4—Important Terms and How to Misuse Them

In today's heated public discourse, it's common for words to be thrown around like so much confetti: "freedom." "Terrorism." "Hurry-up offense." "MySpace sex pervert." But what do these words really mean? It's as if by constant repetition, they've become nothing more than interchangeable symbols deployed for tactical effect by competing sides. In religion, sadly, it's no different, particularly when religion intersects with politics and creates what I call "religiotics." The following will help you avoid looking like a complete damn fool the next time you're blazing away at someone in a chat room about the president's various faith-based initiatives.

remillennialism: This is the belief among some Christians that ever since January 1, 2000, it has no longer been possible, in the words of Prince, "to party like it's 1999." Postmillennialists are those Christians who believe that it will always be possible to do so, while amillennialists believe that in this context "1999" cannot be understood literally but must be read as an allegorical term roughly meaning "a time at which it is especially appropriate to party."

Fundamentalism: You'll probably hear that fundamentalism began in the early twentieth century as an attempt to define the "fundamentals" of the Christian faith. Happily, today we are no longer burdened by such specific meanings. This word actually has no meaning. It's just convenient shorthand to use for things you dislike. Although it's commonly applied in religious disputes, anyone or anything can be a fundamentalist. Kids: Are your parents giving you grief about sneaking away from home to meet up with shady college guys you met on the Internet? Why, that's nothing less than fundamentalist parenting! Ladies: has your man forgotten your birthday yet again this year, only to turn up at the last minute with some wilted flowers and a gift certificate to the Olive Garden? Fundamentalist romancing at its most heinous. And don't get me started on the fundamentalists at Subway, who hear "a little mayo" as "all the mayo it is feasible to use while still calling the sandwich a solid." Actually, that new cheese they have there is pretty fundamentalist, too.

The Emerging Church: A term that refers to churches attended exclusively by white people in their twenties and thirties who have at least one tattoo or body piercing. Their distinguishing characteristics are a refreshing, up-to-date interpretation of Christianity and a reluctance to answer questions directly.

Nicene Creed: This is the Christian Pledge of Allegiance, recited every Sunday in squadron meetings by Christians all over the globe. Adopted in the fourth century at the behest of Emperor Constantinople, it was designed to counter the influence of the Arians, who argued that Jesus was German.

Touchdown Jesus: When professional athletes thank Jesus for helping them win a game, this is the Jesus they're referring to. However, it's not true that Jesus is a fan of one team—how preposterous! No, Jesus is just venting the anti-jock rage he has left over from high school on the other team and delighting in their failures, particularly when those failures occur in a game that would have clinched a pennant if it weren't for some *moron* in the stands reaching out to grab a ball that was still in play. Baseballs are three for a dollar, sir; knock yourself out.

Sex: It's important to clear up a few misconceptions about this term as it applies to Christians. First: It's technically true that Christians are not allowed to have sex. Scientists are not entirely sure how they've managed to grow to the point where there are over two billion of them; it certainly can't be the music. Perhaps they have some kind of deal worked out with the Hindus; we just don't have all the facts.

There's an old joke about Christians opposing sex because it leads to dancing, but anyone who's ever seen the pope spread out some cardboard and bust out his truly jawdropping arsenal of breakdancing moves knows that doesn't hold water.

Theocracy: Webster's defines theocracy as "a situation in which killjoy Christians run the country in such a way that we can't have facial piercings or all-night rave dances anymore."[17] Theocracy is to today's anxious liberals what "fascist" was to their Beatnik parents: a buzzword that has lost all meaning but that sounds good when being shouted through a bullhorn at grimly serious undergraduates gathering to "speak truth to power."

Armed with the above knowledge, you're now ready to take on the world. Whether logging onto a computer or shouting at a relative over Thanksgiving dinner, you have the necessary theoretical ammunition to cut through the white noise and hyperbole about "fundamentalists" and "Hell" and get to the heart of the matter, whatever that may be.

Americans shouldn't let religion divide us. We should let it unite us, as we've let race, ethnicity, class, and gender unite us — as one, diverse people, the devoutly faithful and the just-as-devoutly faithless, the wise Internet Theologian and the utter knucklehead (e.g., Thomas "Everyone Will Be Unitarian" Jefferson) alike.

Christians and atheists aren't as far apart as they imagine. Both groups work hard, pay their taxes, love their children, and celebrate the birth of our Lord and Savior Jesus Christ by taking advantage of spectacular December bargains at the mall. I firmly believe that, armed with the kind of knowledge that flows from this Internet Theologian like a mighty river, Christian Americans and Godless Americans alike can come together and pick a small, insignificant religion to serve as the butt of all our jokes.[18]

---

[17] Conceivably. Who has time to look it up? Especially with so many great viral videos out there to watch.

[18] Everyone seems to like Scientology for this, but my dark horse is Zoroastrianism.

And then—when the last harsh words have been forgotten, when we've forever put aside our conceptual armor and our theoretical weapons, when the Internet is once again an unsullied paradise of fully accurate information and links to blurry photographs of celebrities who forgot to wear underwear—we can look forward to the triumphant realization of our long-held national dream, the prospect that has tantalized and beckoned us for decades:

Ensuring that the New York Yankees never win another World Series.

WHAT JOB CAN TEACH US ABOUT DATING HIGH SCHOOL GIRLS

OR *BIBLE TRANSLATIONS WYCLIFFE NEVER INTENDED*

Among his numerous other achievements, God has always been an "A-list" author.

This dates all the way back to when the Israelites wandered in the desert, when God wrote the Ten Commandments on a piece of stone and gave them to Moses, who promptly broke them. This established a troubling pattern in theological history: the Word of God is often entrusted to the clumsiest among us.

This is also a perfect example of why—putting false modesty aside—the ancient Israelites could have used an Internet Theologian. If God had given such a trusted citizen-scholar the Decalogue on, say, a flash drive, then not only would they not have been broken, but also they would have come with helpful hyperlinks.

Be that as it may, the broken Decalogue illustrates an important point: the written word is at the very center of Christianity, as evinced by the term used by Muslims to describe Christians: "The People of the Book That Is Occasionally Marketed to 'X-treme Teens.'" The Muslims, of course, are referring to the one book essential to Christians, a book without which it is virtually impossible to imagine Christianity at all,[1] a book that forms the very bedrock of the faith of millions.

This book is, of course, *The Da Vinci Code*.

A smaller, older, more irate brand of Christians, though, still swears by the Bible, and it is this trusty tome upon which the Internet Theologian now trains his unshakeably profound gaze.

As hard as it may be to understand, God didn't write the Bible all at once. In fact, some so-called experts insist that God didn't write the Bible at all; rather, they maintain that he "inspired" a group of disparate authors and editors over many centuries to assemble the materials that we call "the Bible." As it happens, some of these "experts" include the authors of the books of the Bible, many of whom selfishly took credit for their work. But, until a better theory comes along, we'll stick with the inspired-multiple-authors thing.

Before we consider the Bible's place in Christianity, it is first necessary to answer a question of utmost urgency: Does God get royalties from sales of the Bible?

The answer to that question is "no," although lawyers for Job are still litigating the matter. But the more pertinent question is this: Just what is the Bible, anyway? And, more importantly, can it really teach me to melt away those unwanted pounds in time for bathing suit season?

As in all areas of modern life, answers to these questions can be found in one place: the Internet. But who has time to look them up when there are so many great reality shows on TV? Answer: the multi-tasking Internet Theologian (me).

---

[1] Despite their having gotten along without it for three-hundred years or so.

THE BIBLE
GOD'S PERENNIAL BESTSELLER

The Bible as we have it today is divided into two parts: the Old Testament and the New Testament. Many scholars feel these terms contain unscholarly value judgments,[2] and so prefer the respective terms: "The Angry God Part" and "The Happy God Part." Because of the Internet Theologian's demonstrated commitment to academia, I'll use those terms.

The Angry God Part was written by a succession of extremely aggrieved Jewish people over the course of several hundred years. This part of the Bible describes how God forges a permanent, everlasting covenant with the nation of Israel, the people he chooses above all others. It also describes, in great detail, the succession of wars, invasions, plagues, disasters, catastrophes, and diet crazes God unleashes upon the nation of Israel. A key theme of this part of the Bible is that God is, at best, somewhat mercurial.

This part of the Bible is divided into several parts: the "Pentateuch,"[3] the Histories, the Major Prophets, the Minor Prophets, the Prophets Who Barely Deserve a Passing Mention, the Wisdom Books, and Record Reviews.

The Pentateuch includes the Torah, the center of the Jewish Bible. These were the books that tradition records were written by Moses, which is certainly possible, given that the books basically make him out to be some kind of big shot. It is in these books that much essential information is imparted, such as the Ten Commandments, which beaked creatures it is okay to eat, and who begat Kenaz.[4]

---

[2] Scholars, remember, have no values.
[3] From the Greek, meaning literally, "Five teuchs."
[4] Eliphaz.

The Historical Books detail Israel's various disastrous attempts at self-government. At several junctures in these books, foreign kings are killed in extremely unpleasant ways.

The Prophetical Books record the thoughts and rantings of ancient Israel's bloggers, the prophets—those merry, locust-eating drifters who tended to show up at moments of severe national crisis to jeer at the Israelites for improperly sacrificing bullocks. Needless to say, these books record that the prophets were distinctly unpopular.

The Wisdom Books contain everything that didn't fit into one of the other categories, including a bunch of songs and the Book of Job, in which God provocatively answers the question of evil with the reply, "Because I'm God, that's why."

The Angry God Part was a bestseller in ancient Israel, but critics agreed it was a bit of a downer, what with all the massacres and lamentings of prophets and so forth. In order to justify a sequel, most people felt that the motif had to become more uplifting, and that's what led to the Happy God Part or, if you insist on being an unreconstructed bigot, the New Testament.

The Happy God Part does not have quite the historical sweep of the Angry God Part, but it does have a payoff for readers in the form of eternal life. This is a much friendlier God than the one we got to know in part one; there, the best thing that might happen to you is that, following the death of your entire family and the destruction of all your property, as you're sitting on a dung heap scratching yourself with broken pottery waiting to die, God might show up and berate you for being depressed.

God is a much better adjusted deity in the second part, and he has a new name: Jesus Christ. The entirety of the Happy God Part is about Jesus Christ, more or less, although there are cameo appearances by other characters.

The Happy God Part, too, is divided into sections, namely Gospels, Paul's Letters, Letters from Other People Besides Paul for a Change, and the Crazy End of the World Book.

The Gospels are four different histories of Jesus, written by, as the Bobby Darin song reminds us, Matthew, Martin, Abraham, and John. The Book of Acts is often appended to the Gospels, since it was written to explain what happened after the Gospels ended, sort of like *After M*A*S*H*.[5]

Paul's Letters were written by a fellow from St. Paul, Minnesota, named Saul of Tarsus. He didn't know Jesus, but he enthusiastically persecuted people who did. One day, Saul was riding his horse when Jesus appeared in a blinding vision and asked, "Hey, what's with the persecution?" Following this, Saul changed his name to Cassius Clay and became the most important early leader of Christianity. He also wrote many important letters, which are collected in this section.

As the world's foremost Internet Theologian, I like to think of Paul as a kindred spirit, a fellow blogger, even. Just as I am faced with the need to combat countless idiocies across cyberspace, Paul spent his time using the written word to correct problems in the early Christian community across the Mediterranean.

There are some obvious differences between us, though. For starters, Paul didn't have the benefit of a cable modem and a sweet new iMac. Additionally, he was never asked to be a moderator of a Christian community on Livejournal—whereas this solemn honor has been

---

[5] You don't remember this show, do you? Sometimes I worry I dreamt it.

bestowed upon me. Despite these deficiencies, though, Paul managed to produce some interesting material, which is quite obviously best illuminated by his worthiest successor, the Internet Theologian.

Paul, though, wasn't the only "pre-blogger" of early Christianity. The Bible is crammed with letters from early Christians, leaving us to wonder if church members did anything at that point other than write letters and get torn to pieces by the emperor's wildebeests.

Finally, the Bible ends on a spectacular note with the Apocalypse of St. John, also known as the Book of Revelation,[6] also known as "Left Behind." This book details the vision of someone who was possibly the author of several other Bible books. In the vision, the author describes the end of the world, the triumph of God over Satan, the communion of saints, and many, many dragons. This book has inspired, intrigued, and exasperated Christians ever since it was written.

Even scholars—a quarrelsome bunch who usually can't agree on anything, not even which type of tweed jacket gets the moldiest—unanimously concur that, to do this book justice, the film version would have to cost at least $100 million in special effects and be helmed by Stephen Spielberg.

THE BIBLE

Brought to You by Rabbis and Greeks

So much for the Bible's contents. Using the finest in Internet search technology, we turn now to the Bible's history, and to the fact that this crucial book was not written all at

---

[6] Or, among innumerable dullards, "The Book of Revelations." There's just one big revelation, folks!

once, and in fact, none of the authors who contributed to it ever thought they were writing part of a single, unitary work at all.[7]

The contents of the Angry God Part were agreed upon by a group of rabbis at the first-century Council of Java, at which they also invented coffee, thereby earning the lasting gratitude of the Internet Theologian. The contents of the Happy God Part took much longer to agree upon; after the end of the first century, Christians spent hundreds of years arguing over what should go in their book.

The heresiarch Marcion, for example, believed the Bible should consist entirely of the Gospel of Luke, some of Paul's letters, and his grandmother's recipe for black-and-blue cobbler. Other heretics went even farther: the Egyptian heretic Valentinus, for example, argued the Bible should consist of only the letter "h."

Fortunately, orthodoxy prevailed, although not before many books were considered for inclusion that ultimately didn't make it. Among these "almost canonicals" were the Shepherd of Hermas, the Didache, the Fragments of Papias, and Run DMC's *King of Rock*.

When reading accounts of disputes over the Bible's contents, most modern audiences are unanimous in thinking one thing: these people were crying out for the services of the Internet Theologian! Alas, I would not be born for nearly two millenia and, besides, online technology was extremely primitive during the Council of Nicea. According to one Web site, the bishops at that famous conference had to make do with primitive electronic bulletin boards rather than full-blown Internet access. No wonder the thing took weeks.

---

[7] This is part of the reason they don't get royalties, of course.

But despite such adversities, the book we know as the Bible was basically in place by the end of the fourth century. And as Christianity spread outside the Greek-speaking world, the Bible went with it, translated into Latin, Frankish, and, eventually, a language invented by Sts. Cyril and Methodius to make dealing with the Russians easier.

This brings us to the question which has bedeviled countless generations of Christians and enriched an equal number of generations of publishers: translating the Bible.

GODSPEAK IN CHATROOM SHORTHAND
TRANSLATIONS OF THE WORD

Initially, the Bible was in either Hebrew (Angry God Part) and Greek (Happy God Part) or just Greek (Angry God Part plus Happy God Part), depending on whether your priest had a beard or not.

Church Leaders, though, eventually decided that the Bible should be available to those who didn't speak Greek, and to this end, St. Jerome the Multilingual issued the Vulgate, a Latin translation of the Bible so named because in it, the prophets are incredibly foul-mouthed.

That act set in motion a chain of events that eventually led, in our time, to the most undeniably influential and widespread of religious texts.

Again, I am speaking, of course, about *The Da Vinci Code.*

No! I'm only kidding. In characteristic cyber-fashion, I have "zinged" you, as well as tried to convince inattentive browsers that this work is a tie-in to that lucrative novel.

What I'm actually referring to is the tendency to

translate the Bible not just into the vernacular tongue,[8] but into dialects of the vernacular tongue, including teenage slang. You see, St. Jerome wrote that "Ignorance of Scripture is ignorance of Christ," and Bible translators have taken it as their goal to make sure the Bible appears in as many versions as possible, so as to leave no human being unreached by the Word of God. If they could find a way to translate the Bible for illiterate people, they would; probably someone is already working on it.

This has led to a veritable Babel[9] of Bible translations, many of which come with covers prominently displaying pictures of young men playing electric guitars. There are Bibles aimed at fans of rap music; Bibles aimed at young career women; Bibles aimed at video gamers; Bibles aimed at restless young men with goatees who play sports that require knee pads and helmets; Bibles aimed at people who pretend to be vampires in their spare time.[10]

There are even Bibles cleverly designed to look, not like Bibles, but like something else: glamour magazines, adventure novels, tasteful furniture. The idea here seems to be to lure unsuspecting young people into picking up a fashion magazine in search of tips on getting rid of bags under their eyes only to have the Word of God smuggled into their consciousness. A few such strategically engineered Bible readings, and the next thing you know — wham! These new young converts are denouncing Israelis for improper bullock sacrifice.

This redesign comes in handy because, let's face it,

---

[8] This was a key demand of the Reformation, but it was opposed by Catholic officials who argued that the Bible in French would sound "snooty."

[9] The word "Babel," of course, comes from the famous episode in Genesis where Jacob wrestles with an angel.

[10] Although I haven't seen such a version. Yet.

"traditional" (read: dull) Bibles are pretty unpleasant objects from an aesthetic viewpoint. Big, black, leather-bound things taking up space on a bookshelf say only one thing about their owner: "I am a morbid weirdo who is right now judging your immodestly exposed forearms."

However, what does a splashy, full-color Bible-flavored magazine say about you? How about a Bible CD-ROM program or a series of animated Bible flip books?

For one thing, these options say, "I am a modern consumer of things biblical and will not settle for a thick, dusty, leatherbound book." They also say, "I have a great deal of discretionary income."

The plain old Bible just isn't good enough for today's flashy, style-obsessed world. Sure, we're constantly told that the Bible is the bestselling book of all time, but who's actually read the thing? What with competition from video games, TV shows, cartoons, and Internet videos of celebrities using incredibly foul language, one wonders whether all those Bibles are doing anything other than sitting untouched inside hotel night stands.

Of course, in presenting Bible text in a radically re-envisioned format, don't today's Jeromes run the risk of trivializing the Scriptures or even of changing their meaning entirely? That's what boring people suspect, anyway.

Just as a "for instance," let's compare a famous Bible verse (John 12:24) as it appears in the King James translation with its translation in the new, hot, contemporary *Biblezine*:

Here's John: "Verily, verily, I say unto you, Except a corn of wheat fall into the ground and die, it abideth alone: but if it die, it bringeth forth much fruit."

Now here's the *Biblezine*: "Q: What should Christians do about downloading music from the Internet? A: If you're on a legitimate Web site that ensures musicians get paid for their music, then go ahead and do it. But stealing music is still stealing, and that's not a page from Jesus's playbook!"[11]

As we can see from this comparison, the doomsayers are exaggerating the danger of situating the gospel in a radical environment; the contemporary version is clearly vastly superior. I mean, who can handle all those "abideths" and "bringeths," not to mention that silliness about "a corn of wheat." Hellooooo! Is it wheat or is it corn? Plus, "fruit"? Um, Johnny, I don't know how to break this to you, but corn and wheat are both *vegetables*. And these guys were supposed to be from an agrarian society.

We, of course, are not an agrarian society. Indeed, it's doubtful whether we're a society in which 70 percent of the population could supply a satisfactory definition of the word "agrarian."

What we are is divided — by ethnicity, by income, by sports team. And just as our modern sages — advertising executives — have determined that we are a nation of niches, so too have the Biblemakers responded and made it their mission that no niche shall go unBibled.

The idea here seems to be that every person gets the Bible he deserves. It makes sense when you think about it: Can you imagine God giving the same Word to you as to those punks down the street who spend all their time skateboarding and listening to music that sounds like a drill sergeant swearing over the sounds of a trashcan being beaten with a sack of soda cans? Of course not. What kind of idiot do you take God for?

---

[11] Technically, this is not the direct translation found in the *Biblezine*. However, this phrase was on the same page as John 12:24 and rendered in a much more attractive font (Internet Theologian Bible Presentation, Lesson One: font matters).

Eventually, the goal is that there will be an edition of the Bible for every man, woman, and child in the world. I, for one, welcome this development and eagerly anticipate a Bible tailored to my personal needs, featuring pictures of things I am interested in[12] interspersed with occasional nuggets of Bible text written in an easy-to-read format without all the "begats" and "Hell."

GOD'S CLUNKY PROSE
The Problem with Scripture

This brings us to another important point: the Bible our parents—and especially our grandparents, the poor shmucks—grew up with is appallingly written. Part of the problem is the material itself: Jesus just couldn't leave the farming metaphors alone. Hey, that's great about wheat and tares and hillocks, but nobody knows what that crap means anymore. People today think in terms of MP3s, reality television, and Internet Theologians. Leave the crop rotation stuff to the "Old Farmer's Almanac," Lord. That's why it's necessary to translate the Bible not just into new languages, but into new dialects.

It was Jesus, of course, who said, "Go forth, preach and make disciples among all nations, even ones with alphabets that look like little squiggly lines." Christians have certainly heeded this instruction, and now the Bible is available in virtually every human language,[13] including those languages spoken only by several hundred members of especially murderous Stone Age tribes, who have no word in their language for "mercy" but who have

---

[12] Fighter jets and bikini models.
[13] And probably in Klingon, too.

fifty-seven lyrical variations of "disemboweled."

That's all well and good, and surely everyone should be able to read the Bible, even people whose only interaction with the wider world is to shoot primitive blow darts at it. But to limit translation only to different languages is to make a serious presumption about what's necessary to get the message across, and as the Bible itself teaches us, "Presumeth not, lest thee abominate thy hillocks" . . . or something.

English versions of the Bible, for example, are generally produced with the assumption that all speakers of English are speaking the same English. Nothing could be further from the truth. In fact, there are many different variations of English, each appropriate to some group, occupational category, or particular subculture revolving around ear-damagingly loud music. And each variation demands its own Bible.

Let's take the most famous example of the Bible in English. The most influential version of Scripture for Anglophones—at least, according to an Internet search I did while waiting for toast one morning—is unquestionably the Authorized Version, more popularly known in America as the King James Version, and even more popularly known as the Bible that uptight English dudes everywhere are always quoting from.

As every schoolchild knows, the King James Version was written by Shakespeare, who was on a brief break from being Christopher Marlowe. As such, it's full of unwieldy Shakespeare-isms like "thee" and "thou" and "slew" and "smote" and "I come not to praise Caesar, but to bury him." This makes it an extraordinarily unwieldy document for anyone who is not comfortable in a powdered wig.

This version, though, is the one all people seem to think of when they think of the Bible, which is somewhat problematic, since scholars now agree that it has so many translation errors that it is technically the holy book of an entirely different religion.[14] More important for the Internet Theologian's purposes, it's where God gets his reputation as being something of a Renaissance *Faire lame-o.*

The King James Version, for example, is where God allegedly says, "Thou shalt not kill," a famous sentence usually quoted by sissy types opposed to violent videogames and suchlike. The problem with this sentence, in modern terms, is that 50 percent of it may as well be in a foreign language. I mean, who talks like this? When was the last time you said, "Honey, doest thou needeth anything from Dunkin' Donuts? I shalt go there for a Coolatta. Doest thou want a croissandwich?"

Now, let's take the same four-word sentence and see what it would sound like coming from, say, Fonzie:

"You buckos better cool it with the killing, and I mean *now*, dig? Heyyyyyyyyy."

Whoah! I don't know about you, but a God who's cool enough to lay it on the line like that can be my deity any day!

We have thus demonstrated both that it's possible to produce the Bible in a visually appealing format (say, a monster magazine) and in a language that's up-to-date, all without doing violence to the essential message of the book. But can we go one step farther? Can we take it upon ourselves to actually *edit* the Bible as we know it?

Prepare yourself for a shocking answer: *We Already Have!*

---

[14] Possibly Zoroastrianism.

GOD NEEDS AN EDITOR

Let's be perfectly honest: the Bible is a long, long book. The Internet Theologian's copy of the Authorized Version clocks in at 971 pages, and that's in what scholars refer to as "wicked small type." And you think that's long? You obviously haven't stomped very long in these particular vineyards, chum. At 971 pages, this is a diet Bible compared to the annotated study copy of the New Revised Standard Version I have, which wraps things up with "Amen. Come, Lord Jesus" on page 2337.

Read that again: 2337!

Think about what that number means: If you started reading this Bible on the day Jesus was born, and you read at a rate of one page per year, *you would now be living hundreds of years in the future!*[15]

Clearly, this is not what Jesus had in mind when he said, "And give to them *brief books* to read, so that they may not grow *weary* with all the chronologies and lists of rules and suchlike."

Okay, he may not have said that, but here's a challenge from the Internet Theologian: prove me wrong. Go ahead. Read the whole Bible through to make sure Jesus doesn't say that. I'll be waiting right here when you report back in 20 years.

The fact is, no one has ever read the whole Bible. Why do you think it was a group of rabbis who determined the contents of the Angry God Part and a group of bishops who did the same for the Happy God Part? The key word here is *group*: that was so a bunch of guys could tackle the

---

[15] Or, more realistically, you would have died roughly 1,960 years ago without having made much of a dent in your reading.

prophets, while another bunch of guys could tackle Paul's incessant letters to the Corinthians.[16] No one—even in the Roman period, a time prior to the invention of TiVo— would have dreamed of reading the whole thing without a team of bearded clerics to help out. I mean, *2337 pages*!

Since no one can possibly read the whole Bible, what we do instead is create our own Bible-within-a-Bible, where we focus on the important parts—like why we're not going to Hell, despite our constant stream of lustful thoughts and visceral dislike of beggars—and forget the unimportant parts, like those obscure passages about rich people being in trouble. This is perfectly natural and normal, and in fact, Christians have been doing it since early days, which is why you rarely see the Epistle of Titus cited by anyone outside Titus's immediate family.

In an Internet era, the Bible-reading public demands a more immediate experience, and in case you missed the message here, the Internet Theologian is explaining exactly why it's okay—even necessary—to market the Bible directly to, say, carnies.

You see, the Bible is not a fixed document menacing us with its canonicity; rather, it's a fluid work waiting to be shaped by each age as it sees fit. The Bible can be repackaged, retranslated, and even redacted, and still remain the Bible.[17] This might not bode well for stick-in-the-mud types who insist that God is irreducibly one way or another, but it bodes extremely well for those wishing to . . . (cue fanfare) . . .

---

[16] Just as an aside, what was it with the Corinthians, anyway? Don't you think Paul probably felt like writing them off? I do.

[17] This discovery gave rise to the popular catchphrase, "No Matter How Thin You Slice It, It's Still Deuteronomy."

MAKE YOUR OWN BIBLE, THE CHEAP AND EASY WAY!

That's right: it's time to apply the wealth of knowledge we've gained in this chapter to assembling our own Bible. Who knows? With a little work and a good marketing push, our Bible just might end up sharing space on bookshelves with abstinence coloring books and skateboarding DVDs all over America.

A critical fact to know about the Bible is that — in contrast to what scholars call "the olden days" — today, anyone can publish their own Bible. You don't have to get God's permission or anything! God's great and all, but he's something of a chump when it comes to copyright law. I mean, the Bible's the most popular book in the world — do you have any idea how much money God has given up by allowing it to enter the public domain? He could probably buy two more Heavens just with the royalties — and that's not even considering merchandise tie-ins!

With the advent of the Internet, publishing a Bible doesn't even require relying on all that clunky technology made famous by actor Steve Guttenberg. You can publish an e-Bible.[18]

The point is, it's a snap to get the thing published. But tread cautiously here. When undertaking Bible publishing, you don't want to publish just any edition of the Bible. You don't, for example, want to break out yet another edition of Shakespeare's Boring Forsooth Version for People in Ruffles, slap it between pastel-colored covers, and hope some professor is enough of a sadist to make his classes buy copies.

---

[18] Although, quite frankly, I advise against it: no one takes e-books seriously. I may be an Internet Theologian and all, but nothing says "crank" like a downloadable book.

That won't work at all. The Bible market is crowded with all kinds of new editions, each with its particular hook. If we want to rise above the other Bibles and satisfy the universal craving to seem erudite without having to work too hard, we're going to need to give the Bible-buying public something they've never seen before.

So let's start with our niche: Who will want to read this Bible? Our readers should be inquisitive and yearning, intelligent and decisive. They should be eager to explore their own ideas about the world, but deferential to the wisdom of the ages. Most important, they should have disposable income and a willingness to be pandered to.

With that in mind, let's craft a Bible for the parents of "cool" Christian kids. That is, the kind of Christian kids who skate, wear "Jesus Is My Homeboy" t-shirts, listen to Christian emo bands, and yearn for a tattoo that says "4HIM 4LIFE." It's imperative that parents of these youngsters seem hip, cool, and with it, and not too much like a bunch of Annotated Study Version dorks. For if they lose that solid bond with their offspring, their kids could end up as aimless junkies, burnt-out wrecks, or even Catholics.

Anxiety being a good market unifier, we've now zeroed in on our targeted readership. Next, we need a come-hither subtitle, something like, "The Word of God for the Parents of Today's Cool Christian Teens." You may think that's patronizing, but trust me, there are people who will read that and think, "That's me! I'm a parent of today's cool Christian teens," and buy two copies. St. Jerome called them "suckers."

We can't call it the Bible, though. "The Bible" is very, very lame. If you are going to write a book called the Bible, it ideally should be anything but the Bible, like a guide to bars in New York City where women with especially low self-esteem can be encountered. The Bible does not say "hip Internet Theologian": it says "Professor Boring of the Institute of Lame-ology."

We'll call our version "What's the Haps," which is a phrase teenagers used about fifteen years ago to mean, "What's happening?" Our target niche will not know that this phrase dates from the end of the Cold War, however, and will think it a perfectly cutting-edge way to describe the Word of God. (Part of our compensation for writing this version of the Bible, as I see it, is that we get to laugh at our target niche.)

So we've got our niche and we've got our name. The next step is to translate the Bible into a language accessible to modern adults while still retaining the essential meaning of the Bible. Here's what I recommend: take a King James Version of the Bible and imagine a hippie Social Studies teacher trying to explain it to a room full of delinquents. Now, start typing.

It's surprisingly easy to translate the Bible, once you have a niche in mind. Our niche is people who are roughly in their late thirties or early forties, so our translation must reflect cultural references that will seem as familiar to them as Jesus' constant references to farming and other boring garbage were to his audience.

Let's try an example, just to show how simple it is. Here's a passage from the short, anguished Psalm 70:

"Make haste, O God, to deliver me; make haste to help me, O Lord. Let them be ashamed and confounded that seek after my soul: let them be turned backward, and put to confusion, that desire my hurt. Let them be turned back for a reward of their shame that say, Aha, aha."

To be honest, I have no idea what the above paragraph says; I lost interest after that pretentious "O God" (it's actually "Oh, God," Shakespeare, Mr. Supposed

Genius) so the remainder was typed by an unpaid graduate student. If that happened to me—a trained Internet Theologian—imagine how off-putting that kind of thing is to the parents of a cool Christian kid.

Ideally, the "What's the Haps" translation of Psalm 70 would skip all that nonsense, instead substituting thematically appropriate lyrics from, say, noted hip hop artist Li'l Wayne or perhaps from Scandinavian popster trio Aha. At last, cool people across America would get to read the Bible as it was meant to be read! Copies of "What's the Haps" would fly off the shelves!

But alas, dear readers, there is a serpent in this particular garden, a serpent known to us Bible experts as Satan. Or, as the serpent is called in court papers, Copyright Law.

America's music publishers are slow to climb aboard the fast-moving Internet-style revolution train called "open source" material. As it turns out, if you quote Aha in your Bible translation, you will soon be visited by a team of burly lawyers who will take objects from your childhood—ones with irreplaceable sentimental value—and crush them right in front of your face.

Therefore, when seeking a suitable translation of Psalm 70, we turn to the safe harbors of the public domain:

> Oh! boat-man haste! The twilight hour is
> Closing gently o'er the lea!
> The sun, whose setting shuts the flow'r,
> Has look'd his last upon the sea!
> A ha! We've moon and star! And our skiff
> With the stream is flowing, Heigh ho!

That's a song by G.P. Morris from the mid-nineteenth century, a time when Americans were prohibited by law from singing or dancing. Instead of being designed to excite the emotions, songs then were principally written to see how many apostrophes could be used.

As you can see, public domain songs do not offer much for today's hip Christian teen.[19] So for "What's the Haps" we'll have to rely on our own fertile imaginations—uh, that is, on our own fertile imaginations guided, as always, by an unerring affinity for quality scholarship.

But the Internet Theologian isn't done yet. There's more to Bible publishing than cribbing old lyrics.

It's all fine and good to find a niche and translate the Bible to suit that niche. But you're not going to translate the whole Bible, because the number 2337 should be keeping you awake with nightsweats. Unless your name is J. K. Rowling Meets Dan Brown and Has Sexy Adventures with a Galaxy of Hollywood's Brightest Stars, no one is going to read your Bible translation once it crosses the five hundred page mark.

What we have to do is edit: cut, chop, slice—but in a godly fashion. Basically, we're taking out all the parts of the Old Testament that don't have sex or violence (bye-bye, Prophets of Boredom!) and most of the New Testament, except a gospel or two, Acts, and that crazy finale. In other words, Marcion was more or less right.

We can't just publish a Bible with only a couple of books, though. Our niche will feel cheated, like they're

---

[19] Nerds will interject here that, as well as songs, the public domain offers a rich treasure trove of some of Western civilization's greatest written works. Dickens, Poe, Melville—all are in the public domain. Our helpful nerd may suggest we plunder those literary pearls for "What's the Haps." Yes, a splendid idea, if the goal is to replace the works of boring, long-winded people with works by people who were even more boring and long-winded. Remember: if it doesn't look good on a bumper sticker stuck to a skateboard, leave it out of the Bible.

not getting the real Bible. If they're going to learn "the haps" on what their kids are doing, they're at least going to want to be able to reference a broad range of Bible books. That's where the Internet Theologian's greatest ally comes in: the summary.

Plenty of Bible "re-imaginings" dispense with the duller books in a page or even a paragraph of summarizing. This is an eminently civilized way to deal with much of the Bible, and one can only wish that God had entrusted his book to people like today's authors, rather than those verbose monomaniacs wandering around in the hot sun he inexplicably chose to favor.

Leviticus, for example, usually takes up between twenty-five and thirty-five pages in most published English Bible versions: it's a long list of instructions on ritual purity given by God to Moses and the Israelites, covering everything from marriage law to food prohibitions. Scholars regard it as one of the most important books of the Old Testament, and it still plays a prominent role in Orthodox Judaism.

Here's how we will summarize it in its entirety:

"God gives Mo' the 411 on snacking."

Got it? Do we need to go on into greater detail? Is your name Maimonides?[20] No? Great. Let's get this thing to a printer and watch as our creation influences the hearts and minds of a mini-niche of a generation.

We've learned a great deal in this space: We've covered the history of the Bible, and we've explored how to make our very own translation, thus teaching a thing or two to early Protestant Reformers, who seemed to think it was some huge deal to translate the Bible.

---

[20] If it is, I apologize for this entire book.

But is it possible to glimpse beyond the present, with its Rap Slang Bibles for Teen Girls on the Go, and look into the future of Bible translation? After all, we live in a bold new era of the Internet and telecommunications that would have seemed impossible to all but our craziest foreparents. As our language changes and reshapes itself according to the new forms of technology available, isn't it inevitable that the Bible will follow accordingly? Is it too much to imagine a Bible written entirely in the language of tomorrow: Internet chatspeak and text message shorthand?

It's not such a shocking future. After all, isn't there room for reinterpretation—and even improvement—on a verse like John 3:5-7 (KJV):

> "Verily, verily I say unto thee, Except a man be born of water and of the Spirit, he cannot enter into the Kingdom of God. That which is born of the flesh is flesh: and that which is born of the Spirit is spirit. Marvel not that I say unto thee, Ye must be born again."

Isn't it just as beautiful, moving, and mysterious when rendered this way:

> JCMSIAH316: POS what r u doin LOL!
> DISIPL23: IMHO :>) WTMIRL???
> JCMSIAH316: :-) ROFL

I don't know about you, but I feel enlightened.

DECK THE HALLS WITH LAWSUITS

Every year, as December 25 draws near, millions of Americans will hear the wondrous story of Jesus' birth. The hasty exit from Egypt, the cold and lonely night in the manger, the shepherds and beasts of the field bowing in acknowledgment of the birth of the promised Savior; all the familiar details will once again become fresh.

This account, drawn largely from the Gospels of Matthew and Luke, is among the most popular tales in all the world, and it marks the occasion of Western society's greatest annual holiday tradition. Concurrent with the religious festivities will be a vast array of customs that have sprung up around the holiday: gift exchanges, houses decorated in colorful lights and sprigs of green, and family newsletters crammed full of bald-faced lies.

Since this annual cycle of customs and the birth they celebrate are so familiar, it stands to reason that most people know the history behind the beloved holiday.

But once again, here we find an illustration of a lesson

the Internet Theologian learns anew each day: reason is no reliable guide.

In fact, few people know much about the holiday celebrated in the English-speaking world as Annual Festive Sale or, sometimes, as Christmas. A recent survey showed that just 8 percent of all Americans can correctly identify Christmas as a celebration of Jesus' birth and not, say, his bar mitzvah (14 percent), confirmation (19 percent), or attainment of a driver's license (a whopping 31 percent).[1]

Ignorance, as it so often does, breeds radio talk show segments and bestselling books by celebrity pundits. It also breeds conflict, and, increasingly, that's what Americans are coming to expect from the holiday season. The so-called "Christmas Wars" pit secular Americans against Christians, Jews against everybody, and Presbyterians against themselves, all in a bitter struggle to define the season's essential characteristics—what it is we're celebrating, why we're celebrating it in December, and just what the heck is "wassailing."[2]

Each year, the tone gets shriller and the reprisals for perceived slights get crazier: one city bans crèches from the town green, so another city installs a twenty-four-hour live Nativity scene in every public school; one store greets shoppers with "Happy Holidays," so another retaliates with "Peace and Blessings upon the Prophet Mohammed and His Family"; one legal advocacy group declares that wearing the colors red and green constitutes a war crime, so another group occupies radio stations and plays Burl Ives's "Have a Holly, Jolly Christmas" around the clock.

---

[1] Note to editor: I will doublecheck these facts before this goes to press. I promise.

[2] It is a type of hat.

So it goes: a never-ending, ever-escalating cycle of rage, recrimination, and banjo-accompanied caroling.

But dear readers, our holidays need not be held hostage by grim politicking. All that's needed to restore the harmony and good tidings that have ever characterized relations between the religious and the secular is a little historical analysis, aided by painstaking yet accessible research into the origins of our holidays and their significance for religious and nonreligious alike.

What we need, in other words, is the Internet Theologian. Lucky for you, I've got all my holiday shopping done[3] and am ready to step up to the plate.

The first thing to note is that Christmas is not the only holiday caught in the struggle between sacred and secular. Increasingly, Halloween, Easter, Thanksgiving, and other holidays are being drawn into the battle. Pretty soon, it will be hard to celebrate any holiday without risking charges of gross religious bigotry; and while "The War on the Feast of the Chair of St. Peter" may not seem as catchy as "The War on Christmas," just wait. Even now, municipalities across America are preparing to scour their town greens for errant miniature papal thrones in the run-up to the big feast.

But if Christmas isn't the only holiday now serving as a subject of tense disagreement among Americans, neither are these holiday battles purely a matter of Christians vs. secularists. These two venerable parties may comprise the main opposing forces, but they've been joined by pagans, Jews, Muslims, Hindus, Jehovah's Witnesses, and the lovable kooks of the Eastern churches, who insist on celebrating holidays on all the wrong days. All these groups

---

[3] Everyone's getting Waffle House gift cards. You're welcome.

have significant claims and counterclaims about major holidays, and the arguments are rooted in the historical and theological complexities of all those denominations, faiths, and sects.

Prime ground, if I may say, for my singular expertise. Let's wade in right up to our elbows, shall we?

HALLOWEEN

Satanic Conspiracy or Chocolate Industry Ploy?

Many Americans do not consider Halloween a major holiday, because no one gets off work that day. This is a powerful and valid argument to make, but it ignores some key points. Arguably, there is more ritual and lore associated with Halloween than with days on which we generally do get to sleep late. Quick—what's the difference between Memorial Day and Veterans Day? Exactly: who cares?

Halloween is another story: dressed in macabre colors of black and orange, and defined by its central ritual of dispensing candy in a vain bid to stave off vandalism, Halloween is one of our most distinctive and festive days of celebration.

But it is also, increasingly, a theological minefield. Adults who remember carefree, bygone Halloweens of dressing in ghoulish costumes and, under the cover of night, collecting candy and playing harmless pranks like smashing the windows of the shop teacher's car may be surprised to learn that Halloween is now viewed with suspicion—even distaste—by a great number of Americans. And not just the weirdos who don't celebrate birthdays; normal people are beginning to question the value of this holiday, and whether it doesn't transmit messages that are fundamentally anti-Christian and even diabolic.

All across America, Christian parents are forbidding children to participate in Halloween activities, or sending them to a church-sponsored "Hell Night," in which they encounter, in a haunted house atmosphere, the horrors of the secular world, like socialized medicine and the unspeakable terrors of the President Hillary Chamber.

Meanwhile, another group of Americans is eagerly seizing on Halloween's growing reputation as Satan's own office party, flaunting what they believe are its un-Christian origins and characteristics. Fueled by sensationalist media accounts, Halloween is quickly becoming as contentious a subject in contemporary America as our ancestors' battle over whether to depict Thin Elvis or Fat Elvis on a postage stamp. Except this time, the gloves are coming off.

The root of the current Halloween dilemma can be summed up in one word: "pagan." This is derived from the Latin word *pagani*, meaning "one who attempts to pull off wearing a cape with a straight face." The word was used by Christian commentators in the ancient world to describe the followers of the many hilarious and impractical Roman religions,[4] but which has since come to be applied, willy-nilly, to virtually any polytheistic faith whose accoutrements can be purchased wherever tarot cards are sold.

Just as was true in the ancient world, today's Christians tend to dislike paganism, although they probably had more grounds back then. I mean, the pagans spent an awful lot of time tracking down and disemboweling Christians,

---

[4] Cult of Mithras, anyone? Seriously: what a bunch of rubes!

whereas today the worst indictment that can be levied against pagans is that they tend to go a little heavy on the eye makeup.

At any rate, Christians consider paganism a bad thing, and therefore anything redolent of paganism is to be avoided.[5]

You might ask what all this has to do with Halloween.

In that case, I might answer that an increasing number of Christians are now shunning October 31 festivities because they are convinced the holiday is itself a pagan custom.

This may come as a surprise to those Americans who, as children, associated it primarily with the Hershey corporation and, as adults, think of it almost solely as an opportunity to see young women dressed as naughty nurses. But, ironically, it's a conviction shared by many Christians and pagans, and one backed up by a great deal of poor scholarship. Exactly the kind of scholarship most appropriate for the Internet Theologian, in other words.

Let's start with what we can consider a representative view. This is presented by, no fooling, the American Folklife Center at the Library of Congress[6]:

> Samhain became the Halloween we are familiar with when Christian missionaries attempted to change the religious practices of the Celtic people. In the early centuries of the first millennium AD, before missionaries such as St. Patrick and St. Columcille converted them to Chris-

---

[5] Pay close attention here, because this will be important later, when we discuss Easter, Christmas, and Flag Day.

[6] Jack Santino, "The Fantasy and Folklore of All Hallows," Online Collections of the American Folklife Center, Library of Congress, September 1982, http://www.loc.gov/folklife/halloween.html (accessed June 6, 2007). See? Research!

tianity, the Celts practiced an elaborate religion through their priestly caste, the Druids, who were priests, poets, scientists and scholars all at once.

Samhain—pronounced "sow-in," because the ancient Celtics were apparently terrible spellers—is the pagan festival of the dead/pagan New Year's Day which was co-opted by crafty Christians looking to rook the Boston Celtics into playing for Rome's team, so to speak. It's not exactly clear why the Celtics celebrated a festival of the dead on the same day as New Year's; perhaps they were an especially thrifty people and were trying to save money on bunting.

At any rate, many of the customs we associate with Halloween actually come from the ancient Celtics:

▶▶ Trick-or-treating comes from the Celtic custom of leaving offerings of food, drink, and Bit-O-Honeys out for the spirits of the dead, who frequently returned at Samhain despite steep holiday fares.

▶▶ Dressing up in scary costumes comes from a related custom of trying to keep the spirits of the dead at bay by frightening them with masks and other strange outfits. This raises at least two important questions: First, why were the Celtics simultaneously offering food to the spirits and trying to scare them away? Perhaps this is why Celtic civilization collapsed. Second, what exactly did they think the spirits of the dead were going to be afraid of? Dying a second time?

▶▶ Bobby "Boris" Pickett's smash hit "Monster Mash" (#1 in 1962) is actually an appropriated version of an ancient Celtic Halloween carol that was, once again, designed either to ward off or attract the spirits of the dead. Also,

Elvis Presley once said it was the most ridiculous song he'd ever heard.[7]

As we can see, the Christians took a lot of the good stuff from Halloween in a bid to convert the Celtics. But, the narrative goes, they weren't as tolerant as all that: the Christian appropriation of Halloween had sinister, underlying motives.

Again, we turn to the Library of Congress:

> Samhain, with its emphasis on the supernatural, was decidedly pagan. While missionaries identified their holy days with those observed by the Celts, they branded the earlier religion's supernatural deities as evil, and associated them with the devil.

This obviously stands in stark contrast to Christianity, with its decidedly unsupernatural focus on miracles, divine communications, and the physical resurrection of the dead.

Upon the Celtics' pagan revelry, the Christians imposed first the concept of All Saints Day, an idea similar to ladies' night at a bar but applying only to saints, and followed it up with All Souls Day, a more egalitarian sequel. The night before All Saints Day was called Hollow Eve, named after the hollowed-out trees where the Celtics would practice free throw shooting. However, the state of dentistry in ancient Celtania was pretty poor, and the mumbling Celtics generally called it something that sounded like "Halloween," which is how the holiday has

---

[7] You may be surprised to learn that the Internet Theologian himself actually heard Bobby "Boris" Pickett relate this Elvis anecdote at a concert held at a fairground in Foxborough, Mass. You will not, however, be surprised to learn that Pickett played "Monster Mash." Twice.

been smuggled down to us, a pagan timebomb ticking away in a black and orange papist wrapper.

At this point, I suppose the elementary sense of fairness imbued in me by my role as Internet Theologian compels me to point out that this view is not accepted by all historians and scholars. Among other things, these terrifically boring people will tell you that:

▶▶ Samhain was neither a New Year's Day nor a festival of the dead. A nineteenth-century Cambridge scholar named Sir John Rhys drew that conclusion by projecting contemporary folk beliefs back into prehistory, in a methodology many historians today would characterize charitably as "the apex of moronic reasoning."

▶▶ Trick-or-treating can be traced to English customs of "souling" or "catterning," holiday occasions, when the poor members of the community would go from house to house asking for special cakes or other delicacies. In pre-Reformation England, the begging was considered helpful in easing the torment of souls in purgatory. The practice was common at virtually every major holiday, not just All Souls Day.

▶▶ As for the costumes, historically it has taken very little prodding to convince the English to dress up in ridiculous garb.[8]

In other words, according to the Boring Patrol, virtually every aspect of Halloween can be traced back to recent history, with many contemporary customs going back no farther than the twentieth century. As you can

---

[8] Have you ever been to Buckingham Palace? It's like Romper Room over there.

imagine, these scholars and historians are not very popular at parties, and with good reason: if they had their way, women probably wouldn't dress up as naughty school superintendents or saucy librarians, children wouldn't revel in ancient pagan mysteries, and instead of bobbing for apples, everyone would sit around and read. It's a darn good thing no one pays attention to these killjoys.

Oh, sure: if you actually "examine documentary evidence" and "search the written sources," you'll find precious little proof for the theory that Christian missionaries appropriated Samhain and formed Halloween, with the pagan features remaining remarkably in tact across fifteen centuries of war, upheaval, economic change, mass migration, and religious conversion.

But if you think that way, you might as well close this book right now, because you're unable to appreciate the special insights of the Internet Theologian, whose credo is: *Facts Can't Stand in the Way When Truth Doesn't Matter.* You'll also have a hard time appreciating all the fun, crazy arguments about Easter and Christmas, to which we now turn our attention.

EASTER

SATANIC CONSPIRACY OR CHOCOLATE INDUSTRY PLOY?

Sometime in the eighth century, an English scholar known as the Venerable Bede wrote that the holiday of Easter was named after a pagan goddess called Eostre, who formerly had been worshiped in the month of April. No other mention of this goddess has ever been found, though, forcing scholars to conclude that Bede's explanation is an interesting idea unsupported by evidence. And there the matter rests.

No! Of course not. The matter never rests, not for a trained Internet Theologian, nor for the numberless legions of axe-grinders and wackjobs with Internet connections. Because of a stray mention in a book written one thousand, three hundred years ago that also contains numerous accounts of magical wells, there is a booming industry in claiming a pagan origin for Easter, the central holiday of the Christian calendar.

You remember the pagans from Halloween? Well, we're talking about different pagans now: specifically, pagans of the Middle East, who worshiped a goddess named Ishtar.[9] Many people have suggested that "Eostre" and "Ishtar" sound kind of similar. And, despite the fact that there's no direct evidence of a Middle Eastern religious practice being imported to Anglo-Saxon Britain, we just can't ignore the similarity, can we? Ergo, Eostre was Ishtar, who was also the Indian goddess Kali, the Greek goddess Aphrodite, and Florence Ballard, the talented, tragic member of the original Supremes.

In one of those strange team-ups that make theology so compelling, pagans and holiday-scorning Christians alike claim that virtually everything we do at Easter can be traced back to the worship of Ishtar. Hot cross buns, colored eggs, a fixation on rabbits, marshmallow Peeps, and even avoiding the white licorice jelly beans all have their roots in ancient pagan practices. For pagans, this means Christians are suckers for celebrating their holidays with pagan customs; for holiday-scorning Christians, it means

---

[9] Although, to be sure, they certainly did not worship a film named "Ishtar."

the only thing "Christian" about the holiday is the fact that no stores are open.

In fact, one of the central convictions about Christian holidays in popular culture — an idea that has become so widely accepted it's often passed along in newspaper accounts, popular histories, and classrooms as if it were fact — is the idea that the Christians stole everything from the pagans.

You name it, it came from the pagans: chocolate bunnies, Halloween costumes, wassailing[10] — right down to the idea of a God resurrected from the dead, it all came from the pagans. A holiday will not pass without someone you know speculating on the pagan origins of a custom; occasionally, these people will cite a letter that a particular pope supposedly wrote to an English missionary (for which our source is, again, the Bede-Man).

I've done a lot of combing — I've read both the Wikipedia *and* the Answers.com entries on Easter and have reached a conclusion that may shock and inform you, and that will certainly set "mainstream" scholars to tearing out their graying tufts of hair and wailing piteously in their seminar rooms. Here it is:

The Christians did steal just about everything in their religion, but not from the pagans. *They stole it from the Jews.*

FACT: The early church spent decades debating about the best way to set a date to commemorate Jesus' crucifixion and resurrection. They ultimately settled on fixing the date to match as closely as possible a pre-existing holiday — *the Jewish celebration of Passover!*

---

[10] Which, of course, is a method of sledding.

FACT: In virtually every language in the world except German and English, the word for "Easter" is a derivative of the Hebrew "Pesach." Thus, in Latin it's called *Pascha*, in Italian *Pasqua*, in Spanish *La Pascua*, and in Greek, *Paskha*. And when Hebrew speakers say "Pesach," what they really mean is "Passover"—*a known Jewish holiday!*

FACT: Some Christians are so open about their brazen appropriation of an existing religious tradition that they even claim that Jesus—the founder of Christianity— was related to a number of Jewish people, including his mother and stepfather. These people even insist that many early Christians were themselves Jews, despite the obvious contradiction. Which is it, people? *Were they Jewish or were they Christian?*

To their credit, the Jews have been tremendously good sports about the whole thing, not drawing attention to this act of culture piracy, which invariably overshadows the annual celebration of Passover. I'm sorry to have to blow the lid off a cherished myth of pagan appropriation, but in this case, painstaking research leads me to one inescapable conclusion: the Christians are a bunch of wannabe Jews.

We'll have to bear this pathbreaking example of Internet scholarship in mind as we tackle the Mount Everest of holiday donnybrooks: Christmas itself.

CHRISTMAS
SATANIC CONSPIRACY OR CHOCOLATE INDUSTRY PLOY?

Here's a fun Christmas activity the whole family can enjoy: when you're out shopping in December, preparing to "rush home with [your] treasures," as the song has it, stop your busy to-ing and fro-ing when a stranger says, "Happy holidays." Instead of acknowledging the greeting with a grunt and moving on, look them straight in the eye and say, "And Merry Christmas to you." Now, wait and see if he punches you in the face.

Such an exchange would have been baffling to Americans as recently as twenty years ago, but in today's more intelligent, sophisticated society, we are used to belligerent insults exchanged over seasonal greetings. All over the country, from the end of November to the last week in December, decorations are removed, companies are boycotted, lawsuits are filed, and eggnog is consumed,[11] all in the festive revelry we've come to call "The Christmas Wars." Indeed, it seems that if there's one thing Americans enjoy even more than Christmas, it's fighting about Christmas.

At stake are crucial questions about the holiday itself, obviously, but also about Christianity, and the extent to which its practices are influenced or even determined by popular culture. And, because it's a holiday, there's also a bunch of pagan stuff to sift through.

It's important to note at the outset that Christmas was not always so contentious. In the past, tensions over the holiday were usually between Christians and non-Christians, as the latter group felt a slight twinge of exclusion when virtually every store in the country had giant

---

[11] Technically, eggnog consumption is not part of the conflict over Christmas, but it's just as irrational. Have you ever checked the calorie content of a glass of the nog? And I'm sure you can get food poisoning from that stuff. Not for nothing did Martin Luther call it "the devil's very broth." If he didn't actually say that, I'm sure he would have if he had a chance.

signs promoting sales "To Honor the Birth of the One True Lord and Savior Jesus Christ, Whose Might Sunders the Faithless." Looking back, non-Christians probably had a point, however minor.

A happy compromise was reached in 1955, when Congress passed a law creating the basis for non-Christian equivalents of year-end holidays, starting with Hanukkah,[12] the Jewish Christmas. Later, laws were passed creating Eid, the Muslim Hanukkah; Kwanzaa, the Sixties Hanukkah; and Three Kings Day, or *Hanukkah en Espanol*. For a while, America was at peace, joyfully celebrating Christmas and other, lesser holidays. But the amity would be short-lived.

Since the turn of the century, a growing number of Americans have asserted that, not only do they want nothing to do with Christmas, but they don't want to celebrate Hanukkah, Eid, Kwanzaa, Three Kings Day, or Thanksjupiter, either. This strange new breed of holiday-hating American was called the Puritan.

Just kidding. The Puritan was a type of American who also hated Christmas and other holidays, but—as if this makes any sense—for religious reasons.[13] No, the new foes of Christmas were like the Puritans, but without the religious beliefs. They were Ardent Secularists.

The Ardent Secularists insisted that it was an affront to their constitutional rights to be wished a "Merry Christmas," to stand beneath mistletoe, to hear bells ringing, and even to dash through the snow in a one-horse open sleigh. They wanted nothing to do with Christmas and, this being

---

[12] Pronounced "Chanukah."

[13] Not surprisingly, the Puritans were Calvinists. Again, we return to the Internet Theologian's Religion Rule #1: Calvin was a nut.

America, they were prepared to go to court over it.

As a compromise, they proposed saying "Happy Holidays" or "Season's Greetings" or "It's Winter" in lieu of the offensively God-y "Merry Christmas." Immediately, millions of Christians, who had been saying "Happy Holidays" and "Season's Greetings" to each other for decades, suddenly reacted to those salutations as if you were burning crosses in their front yards. Christians and organizations claiming to represent them not only began demanding more overtly religious displays in December, but they also threatened stores, schools, and municipalities that seemed deficiently Christian in their acknowledgment of the season. And, this being America, they were prepared to go to court over it.

Today, it is difficult to celebrate any sort of holiday in December without retaining legal counsel. In response, the dwindling band of Americans who believe in compromise have proposed a way through the holiday impasse, variations of which can be relied upon to pop up in the editorial pages of *The New York Times* sometime around December 23 every year.

The compromise goes like this: Christmas is both sacred *and* secular, so there's plenty for *everyone* to enjoy, except, obviously, Jewish people. The holiday has blended religious and profane traditions so thoroughly that it's impossible at this point to tell which is which, so we should all just go ahead and have a good time. Besides, isn't the whole thing based on pagan customs, anyway?

Ah, the pagans again. At some point during the holidays, you're bound to hear that holly and mistletoe are pagan holdovers; that gift-giving was bequeathed to us by the Druids; that the date itself was chosen by the early church to compete with the Roman Saturnalia; and that

Santa Claus was originally a Siberian shaman figure who is said to wear red and white because Siberians would gut reindeer and wear the skins inside out.

Now, all of these assertions are true insofar as we understand "true" to mean "false." The Roman Saturnalia, for example, actually ended no later than December 23, rather than December 25.[14] And the modern concept of Santa Claus derives almost wholly from a poem written in 1822 by an Episcopal bishop in New York named Clement Clark Moore called "A Visit From Saint Nicholas."[15] The rest of Santa lore seems to come to us from racist newspaper cartoonists, Coca-Cola ads, and World War II propaganda about the dangers of venereal disease.

But the myth of pagan origins is important for those seeking a compromise between the bitterly opposed forces of Christian and secularist when it comes to Christmas. The pagan story allows these folks to say, "Look, it's not a Christian thing or a secular thing—it's a Siberian deer-murdering thing! So let's stop this fussing and get at that eggnog!"

With all apologies to the pagans, they can't take credit for this holiday.[16] This comes down to whether Christmas is a celebration of the birth of mankind's only savior or a chance to wheedle an iPod out of your parents. And so, it

---

[14] For this and many other actual details about holidays, I have relied on the work of Ronald Hutton, particularly his magnificent *Stations of the Sun*. Readers are warned, though, that with too many more of these citations the present volume will be an actual work of scholarship.

[15] Much more famously known by it's opening line: "How the Grinch Stole Christmas."

[16] Pagans can be cheered by the knowledge that they can take credit for lots of genuine, terrific holidays, such as the Fourth of July and Arbor Day.

seems, our holiday seasons from now until the sun blows up are doomed to an endless cycle of conflict, recrimination, and televised shouting matches between lawyers.

That is, of course, unless we all take heed of the Internet Theologian, whose familiar, yet still shocking, counterintuitive conclusion just might blow the stovepipe hat off your snowman:

Christians aren't actually celebrating Christmas.

While this may come as a shock to Christian partisans of the Christmas wars, my research reveals it's an undeniable fact. And get ready to be further shocked and informed: Christmas, like its Jewish spinoff Hanukkah, actually lasts for twelve days rather than one.

It's true. For centuries, Christians all over the world celebrated Christmas starting on December 25—and ending on January 6, which they called "Twelfth Night," to remind themselves that in the morning it wouldn't be Christmas anymore. In fact, a small, obscure group of Christians known as the Eastern Orthodox still celebrate Christmas this way—and preliminary accounts suggest a number of rogue Catholics also follow the old, twelve-day calendar.

A panoply of religious associations were linked to each day of the celebration, with mysterious-sounding names like "St. Stephen's Day" and "Holy Innocents Day" whose meanings are now lost in the mists of time. For some reason that my research was unable to clarify, lots of Christians stopped celebrating all twelve days starting around 1517 or so. Maybe it was a marketing thing; maybe a union lost a strike or something. I can't really tell.

The point is, in traditional terms, Christmas is a party that starts at midnight on December 25 and ends at 11:59 p.m. on January 6. The entire month of December before

Christmas is not "Christmastime" at all; it's actually something called Advent,[17] during which Christians are supposed to fast, pray, and give money to charity. I know, I
know: it sounds insane, right? Who in their right minds
would fast, pray, and give money to charity during the
busiest, most exciting shopping season of the year?!

The more I researched, the more I realized that our
contemporary Christmas celebration is largely a product
of the Victorian middle classes, who sought to distance the
holiday from its religious roots largely because they hated
hugging strangers.

So-called "age-old" traditions like Christmas trees and
greeting cards actually can be traced back to the emotion-
ally distant stiffs of the Victorian Age. For example: gift-
giving. Nothing says "Christmas" like giving each other
presents (except, perhaps, for the local school board's fear
that announcing "winter holidays" in December will bring
a round of lawsuits). But giving gifts to family members
was virtually unheard-of until the Victorian Age!

You see, gift exchanges used to be primarily for members of different classes or occupational categories. The
king would get presents from the lords, who would get
presents from lesser landholders, who would get presents
from serfs, who would get presents from extremely poor
serfs, who didn't get any presents at all and occasionally
rose up and attacked everybody with pikes because of it.
Gift exchange was a stiff and formal gesture not fit for the
warmth of the family circle.

But in the Victorian Age, parents began to spend most
of their time outside the home—inventing steam power,

---

[17] From the Latin *adventus*, meaning, "to slash prices to
record lows."

conquering Africa, growing elaborate moustaches, and that sort of thing. Family members began to seem like little more than people living under the same roof who adopted the same surname for tax purposes. Finally, it got to the point where the familial bonds were so awkward and formal that gift-giving became an appropriate gesture. Doesn't that make you want to run out and buy Dad a necktie?

The Christmas Wars come at an auspicious time. For many years, Christians have been whining about the commercialization of the holiday, even as ardent secularists whine about having to look at a word which contains the letters "C-H-R-I-S-T." But here's the thing: we're actually talking about two different holidays, one sacred and rooted in ancient Christianity, and the other secular and rooted in the peculiarities of nineteenth-century industrial culture.

So, in the spirit of Hanukkah, the Internet Theologian proposes a compromise: ardent secularists and anyone else who likes giving and receiving presents, drinking eggnog, and dashing through the snow, can celebrate the holiday that starts with the Macy's Thanksgiving Day Parade and ends on December 25. In a good-faith gesture, Christians should even consider letting them use Santa Claus as their god for the season.

Christians, meanwhile, will go back to celebrating their twelve-day Christmas blowout starting on December 25, and will prepare for that monster party by fasting, praying, and giving money to the shabbily-dressed Santas who watch the kettles for the Salvation Army.

This is not only a workable solution, it's a way to enjoy the holiday without recourse to lawyers, shouting, or books with titles like *Nativity under Siege: The Plot to Destroy*

Christmas. "Season trees" will dominate town greens before December 25; manger scenes after. Eventually, everyone will realize their differences are tiny in the great scheme of things and will join together in a spontaneous song of joy and friendship that will light the holiday season with its cheer.

And then, at last, we can turn our attention to eradicating eggnog forever.

NUMBER ONE SONG IN HEAVEN

The scene is a vast 4-H field somewhere in our nation's heartland.[1] It is midsummer, and the blazing sun is just now setting, a great orange disc bathing the field and the trees around it in its warm, embracing glow. All around me, young people strain to see what's happening on the stage some three hundred feet away from us.

On that stage stand five young men who could be described as clean-cut except for the large, notable tattoos covering their arms. They have been playing music for about ten minutes to an increasingly rapturous reception from the crowd. Now, during a pause between songs, the lead singer squints out over the monitors on stage, shielding his eyes from the declining sun's glare. He looks out into the crowd, as if searching for something undefinable yet something he'll know the moment it catches his eye. The moment is pregnant with desire, desire for him to say something meaningful, something that will reach

---

[1] If Pennsylvania counts as our nation's heartland.

93

the multitudes of young people who have come to hear him sing.

Finally, after what seems like an eternity, he clears his throat to speak. The crowd is hushed; the moment electric.

"I just want to say . . ." he begins tentatively. The crowd leans forward, hanging on his every syllable. "I just want to say that we have shirts and stuff for sale at our table near the burrito stand." Then he adds, "This next song is about standing firm for Jesus."

And with that, the band launches into another song, and the crowd becomes a frenzy of churning limbs and digital cameras held aloft.

The occasion in question was one of innumerable Christian music festivals held around the country, featuring vast lineups of popular, successful bands and artists whose names and music are probably unfamiliar to most Americans. In fact, so numerous are these festivals that I can't for the life of me remember which one this was: the Praise 4Him Fest? Or possibly the 4Him Praisefest? All I know for sure is that Ozzy Osbourne was not on the bill. Otherwise, it's kind of a blur.

Field research is strange territory for the Internet Theologian, who normally prefers to roll up his sleeves and get his hands dirty the old-fashioned way: by doing Google searches for words like "Theotokos" in the privacy of his own home. Years of research have convinced me that "the real word" is vastly overrated. Indeed, there's very little in the outside world that can't be learned on the Internet, and there's the added bonus that it rarely rains in the room where I keep my computer.

But in recent months, I've been drawn to a number of Christian rock concerts, determined to see exactly what makes these squares tick. More importantly, I wanted to get to the bottom of an industry that now grosses approximately eight kazillion dollars per year,[2] surpassing the amount of money Americans spend annually on cock fight wagers, non-alcoholic beer, and Ice Capades tickets *combined*.

Yes, Christian music is big business; but is it good business? More importantly, is it the kind of business that helps young people gain a better appreciation for their faith, or is it merely a way for Christian parents to feel good about their child blowing hundreds of dollars a month on CDs and downloaded ringtones? I was determined to find out, no matter how many free festival tickets my editors needed to score for me.

At the outset of my journey, I had to acknowledge a significant observation: Christians seem to be the only major faith with a booming musical subculture.

Why is it that only Christianity has spawned an industry raking in millions of dollars by basing faith-centric lyrics on the conventions of popular song? Where are the Jewish rappers? The Muslim heavy metal bands? How many Zoroastrian bands are there?[3]

To find these answers, I would have to dig deep and research long and hard. I would have to interview countless people, do hours of field work, and be willing to investigate strange, out-of-the-way subjects I had never before encountered.

So, instead, I limited myself to the Christian musical culture, which is remarkable for its helpful and plentiful Web sites.

---

[2] Note to editor: I will find the real number before this goes to press.

[3] One: Queen.

Christian pop music may seem like an obvious move: after all, Christians are entering the worlds of video games, movies, theme parks, and marital aids,[4] clearly embracing the trappings of secular culture in a bid to claim some of it for their faith. Music, as one of the most prominent outposts of popular culture, is therefore an ideal place to start when it comes to Christianizing the market. But the history of Christian rock in reality is fraught with bitter controversy, accusations of diabolism, and unspeakably bad haircuts. Let's don our metaphorical backstage passes and have a look, shall we?

GOODNESS, GRACIOUS, GREAT BALLS OF DISAGREEMENT

In the beginning, musical divisions were clear. There was sacred music and there was secular music. Sacred music was basically a bunch of monks chanting, and secular music was basically operas about Vikings killing each other. This worked well for two thousand years, until the invention of the record industry.

Thomas Jefferson, the "Monticello of Menlo Park," not only invented Virginia and the Declaration of Independence, he also brought us the light bulb and the wax platter that posterity has called the "record."

With the record's invention, people for the first time could hear music played in their homes without worrying about fiddlers tracking mud on their carpets. This created a tremendous appetite for recorded music, and soon companies were scouring the country in search of new sounds for their voracious customers.

---

[4] Seriously! Do some checking on the Internet. Not at work, though.

One of the most prolific areas of the country turned out to be the American South, where Scotch-Irish and African traditional musics had spent centuries mixing and blending, creating sophisticated, beautiful hybrids that were distinctly American. With the kind of sensitivity that typified the age, the record companies divided all Southern music into two categories: "race music," played by black people, and "hillbilly music," played by hillbillies.

The real division in Southern music, though, wasn't racial so much as religious. Before radio, widespread concert tours, and video games with soundtracks, the most important forum for music all across the South was the church. The musical traditions of Southern churches were often more robust and vernacular than the staid hymns familiar to congregations elsewhere in America; starting at the turn of the century, with the Pentecostal revival sweeping through the country, churches would even be the scenes of frenzy familiar to later rock concerts, with worshippers leaping and dancing as the sacred songs were played.

Understandably, though, musicians didn't always want to play songs about religion. Sometimes they wanted to sing about things that were important to them in other aspects of their lives, such as drinking too much and having sex with prostitutes. Not surprisingly, this was frowned upon by many church authorities, and the sacred-secular split in Southern music was born.

All this would be merely regional musicological history if it weren't for the fact that all American popular music—and, therefore, all postwar popular music everywhere, even in backwards European countries where people still unironically enjoy heavy metal—is rooted in the vibrant, raucous musical traditions of the American South.

One of those traditions, needless to say, is the extreme suspicion with which religious people viewed secular music. Many early pioneers of rock and roll—musicians like Elvis Presley, Jerry Lee Lewis, and Puff Daddy—got their first exposure to music in the charismatic churches of the South. When it came time to play songs they traditionally had been warned against, many of them were tormented by the paradox of their musical backgrounds and futures. This tension grew after rock and roll suddenly became the most popular music in the country and then in the world, when the style's surge in visibility led some people to denounce the new sound as "the Devil's music."

This longstanding epithet has appeared again and again in popular culture, embodied in such bits of conventional wisdom as "the Devil has all the good tunes"[5] and "Christian rock is abysmal." The idea that the Devil has all the good tunes, frankly, is deeply objectionable to anyone who has ever sat through a recording by a Norwegian Satanic "Black Metal" band, but the Internet Theologian digresses.

The point is that from the birth of rock and roll in the early 1950s, Christians viewed the music with deep wariness, and their suspicion only deepened in the late 1960s, when rock musicians grew out their hair, dressed like Gypsy choruses in comic operetta, and began raging against everything traditional in society, from God to

---

[5] Actually, the relationship between music and the Devil is noted at least as early as the nineteenth century when the Rev. Rowland Hill argued that the Devil should not have all the good times. See the *Oxford English Dictionary of Quotations*, 2nd ed. (London: Oxford University Press, 1966), 248.

signage.[6] The link between Satan and popular music was thus cemented in the minds of many Christians.

But then a strange thing happened. A bunch of hippies who had taken all the acid they could get their grubby fingers on started to become disillusioned with the nihilism of the counterculture and started searching for greater meaning in their lives. However, being hippies, they didn't want to give up the aspects of their lives they enjoyed, such as beards and sandals and inedible vegetarian chili. In an historic act of compromise, many hippies joined Evangelical Protestant ministries, adopting the Christian ethos while maintaining a countercultural appearance. After all, they reasoned, weren't Jesus and the Apostles the *original* hippies?[7] Thus, the Jesus Movement was born.

Although it's inadvisable to make sweeping generalizations about something as complex and decentralized as the Jesus Movement, the Internet Theologian had never been stopped by the need for precision before, and he won't be hindered now. The central idea of the Jesus Movement was that the best way to reach young people with the message of Christ was to speak to them in ways they could understand. Most importantly, this meant appropriating popular culture for Christian purposes. It was essentially an argument that content trumped form: the acid rock dirges of the counterculture could be made suitable for Christian purposes if godly people replaced the antisocial lyrics about the oppression of reading signs with hard-hitting lessons about Jesus and his role in our lives.

The Southern gospel musicians who so scorned the

---

[6] There really is a song protesting the existence of signs. In just a few more decades, the hippies will seem more baffling to us than the ancient Incas.

[7] No; they weren't.

secular world would have been shocked by this development. But then, they lived in a world where it was okay to have a marketing category called "hillbilly," so they probably would have been shocked by a lot of things in the 1970s. And it was at the end of that decade that Christian rock — an unheard-of category just ten years earlier — first gained national prominence, with the public conversion of famed folkie Robert "Bob" Dylan, who went on to record several Christian rock albums that were almost universally despised by non-Christians,[8] who derided Dylan's conversion to such a furious extent that it took Christian rock another decade to emerge from the rubble.

When it did, it was with an entirely new methodology. Instead of laying siege to the mainstream, Christians decided to create their own network of musicians, record labels, shops, performance venues, and radio stations. This paralleled an overall approach to popular culture in Christian circles, which is why today you're able to watch Christian wrestling matches in venues around the country.

This Christian counterculture — which, ironically, has been far more successful in remaining free of mainstream control than anything the hippies ever came up with — is now the standard for Christian pop culture. It has its own superstars, masterpieces, and triumphs, the vast majority of which are known to millions of initiates but completely foreign territory to most other Americans.

As successful as it's been, today's Christian rock scene isn't free of tension. A number of successful Christian performers have "crossed over" to the mainstream,[9] just as

---

[8] Their loss: "Shot of Love" is a masterpiece.

[9] Including, surprisingly, a plurality of gangsta rappers recording today. They crossed over en masse, the short-lived "Shooting Suckas for Jesus" trend having been received with disdain in Christian circles.

did early rock and roll performers like Sam Cooke. And just as in Sam Cooke's day, this has left the original Christian fans feeling angry and betrayed.

Within Christian music circles, too, are persistent doubts about the wisdom of the counterculture approach. After all, the filthy hippies who started the Jesus Movement and integrated rock and roll into Christianity did so with the explicit intention of bringing non-Christians into the fold. Is there value, today's Christians wonder, in creating a large and sustaining but essentially self-contained underground that rarely reaches out to the unconverted? And, furthermore, why do festivals have to charge five bucks for a bottle of water? It seems like Christians should be a little more neighborly, if you catch my drift.

These are questions which preoccupy the world of Christian music. But out in the more hectic realm known as the wider world, there is one overriding question with regard to Christian music, a question that must be met head-on sooner or later:

Why is Christian music so awful?

THE LOST ART OF MAKING A JOYFUL NOISE

Let's not mince words: when most people hear the words "Christian music," they think of one of two things: either a bearded hippie sitting in lotus position, strumming an acoustic guitar and gently singing "Kumbaya," or Pat Boone.

By all accounts, Pat Boone is a wonderful man, and the bearded hippie probably isn't a terrible guy either. It's just that their music has been used in laboratory tests to cure insomnia. It is music you can only imagine being played softly in the background on a Sunday afternoon at your maiden aunt's home in 1975. You can just see it, can't you? It's a spring day and you're yearning to be outside, playing. But instead you're inside, the soft acoustic tinkle coming from the small Dansette record player, and your only relief contained in a glass bowl full of butterscotch discs. You shudder just thinking about it, don't you?

These stereotypes are so widespread, so ingrained, that the words "Christian rock" are virtually a punchline unto themselves.

Baffling, when you consider the rich history of Christian music, even Christian popular music. I defy anyone to listen to a vintage 1950s recording of the Rev. Julius Cheeks performing with the Sensational Nightingales and not come away transformed. Most of the early giants of rock and roll and soul music had church backgrounds, and they frequently revisited their earlier, sacred material. For crying out loud, it's called "soul" music!

Yet the image of Christian musicians as bland, clueless naïfs persists. Ask any professional (or, on the Internet, profoundly amateur) music critic what they think about Christian rock, and you will be met with denunciations of a passionate invective usually seen only in public speeches in far-flung totalitarian regimes. Indeed, in an era when critics pride themselves on "post-rockist"[10] discoveries of such previously scorned genres as country, female-fronted R&B, and the throat singing of the Chilean tree people, Christian music is still universally considered to be radioactive.

If the response is this vitriolic among the godless hordes of rock critics, it's only slightly less so among non-

---

[10] This is a real term that rock critics use. Somebody did a term paper on critical theory and wants to show off!

Christian music fans. These gentle folks are generally only comfortable with references to religion in the form of the oddly respectful mentions of God in rappers' Grammy acceptance speeches. For these thrill-seekers, "Christian rock" has roughly the same appeal as "sugar-free candy": it's a regrettable imitation product appropriate only for people suffering from some kind of imbalance.

Honestly, there is nothing more odious to the secular listener than the prospect of sitting through an evening of Christian music. Hand in hand with their dislike of the actual music, though, is a visceral aversion to being "proselytized"[11] in any way. Secular music fans absolutely resist the idea that music could be a venue for making converts to religion, though they don't resist the similar notion that popular music is a venue that enables, say, the Rolling Stones to evangelize about the superior quality of Jovan Musk.

The Christian reaction to secular disdain is, understandably, to go on the defensive, particularly when faced with anyone who uses the term "rockist" with a straight face. The Christian music fan will point out the tremendous variety of contemporary music made by Christian artists. Gone are the days of the bearded hippie intoning "Michael, row your boat ashore" on the floor at Sunday school. In his place are diverse ranks of Christian goths, Christian punks, Christian indie rockers, Christian "freak folkies," Christian rappers, Christian R&B crooners, and even Christian death metallers.[12] With such a variety of styles, the Christian music fan will ask, what grounds do

---

[11] Secular fans think "proselytize" has a distinct whiff of science fiction about it, like "vaporize," and that Christians actually want to shoot them with ray guns.

[12] True!

people have for turning up their noses at this vibrant art form?

In other words, Christians argue, their subculture is just as diverse and engaging as the secular realm it mimics. Indeed, Christian music fans will maintain that the only way you can tell top artists apart these days is by reading their tattoos.

To test this thesis, the Internet Theologian has delved deep into the vast research capabilities of the World Wide Web and downloaded a representative cross section of songs from a broad array of Christian artists. And, in the spirit of both research and Christianity, the Internet Theologian paid for these legally acquired downloads (although he fully intends to write them off as a business expense).

Here are some of my research notes, presented for the edification of the reader, but also just in case anyone in the Audits department of the Internal Revenue Service questions the merit of the one hundred dollar write-off for iTunes.

TRACK 1: "Awesome God" by Insyderz: This is a Christian ska band. Ska is a form of music invented in Jamaica that is similar in some ways to American rhythm and blues. Outside Jamaica, ska tends to be the only way high school band geeks get to play in the kind of bands that would attract girls. After all, what else are you going to do with your trombone skills? One key element that all non-Jamaican ska bands have in common is the attempt to work the word "ska" into words that would otherwise be ska-less. This song qual-

ifies, because it comes from an album called *Skalleluia!*
Other acceptable uses in a Christian context would be:
"skanctified," skapostles," and "the Nicene-Skanstan-
tinoplian Creed." This is not a terrible song; I would
not object if it were playing while I was doing some
vacuuming around the apartment. But it's hard to follow the argument the band is making beyond the constantly repeated phrase, "My God is an awesome God."
This underlines the problem with ska as an evangelizing tool: after the third song, it all starts to sound the
same, and the mind wanders. This is why, for example,
most Christian hymns were written in waltz time well
into the fifteenth century. A further note: I believe the
correct spelling should be "Insiders"?

TRACK 2: "Casimir Pulaski Day," by Sufjan Stevens.
This artist is the leading member of a genre called
"Excellent Indie Rock that Makes Regular (Read:
Secular) Indie Rock Fans Feel Intensely Nervous," or
EIRMRRSIRFFIN for short. He's achieved a kind of
fame that eludes most Christian artists, and has become
a pin-up for the kind of young woman who dreams of
moving to Brooklyn and running into the Shins on the
subway. Do the Shins even live in Brooklyn? [13] At any
rate, what's funny is that all the reviews and secular
fans of this guy go out of their way to state that his is a
"nonjudgmental, inclusive, and tolerant brand of Christianity," despite there being no indicators whatsoever in
his music about what kind of Christian he is. He could

---

[13] Note to self: research Shins' location before going to
press.

be a Calvinist,[14] for all you can tell from his music. I'm not sure what it is about Christian musicians that makes non-Christians feel they have to spend time reassuring themselves that the artist they like doesn't actually, you know, really *believe* any of that stuff. No one ever makes that kind of effort with, say, Bob Marley, and his religious beliefs were significantly more challenging than those of the average Presbyterian. At any rate, this song, an examination of faith in the face of death, is significantly better than most music that gets played between innings at minor league baseball games.

TRACK 3: "Tell Me What You Think of God," by Story Side B. The popular stereotype about Christian rock is that it's written and played by people who really have no idea what secular (or "real," in common parlance) rock music sounds like. This song is a good refutation of that. In sound, it is indistinguishable from any of the catchy, midtempo rock songs you may hear in a beer commercial, or at a bar, or coming out of the car in line behind you at the Wendy's drive-thru at 1 a.m. Additionally, the members of this band have the look down: from the cover of their album, they appear exactly like the sort of rough-and-tumble young hooligans who make the mall such a traumatic experience for old people. I also give them credit for not pussyfooting around the message, as so many Christian rock bands do; the title is pretty straightforward, after all. And it's an invitation to dialogue: much less popular would be a

---

[14] In that case, of course, he would be a nut.

hectoring song called "I Will Tell You What I Think of God, and You Will Shut Up and Listen."

TRACK 4: "Pondered," by Triggs. One of the great indicators of the ongoing generation gap is what I call "the rap divide." Baby boomers like to pride themselves as the arbiters of all that is hip, and tend to think they have kept their finger on the pulse of pop culture for, oh, six decades now, but they just don't get rap. If a group of young African-American men pulled up alongside a boomer's car blaring this song, it would undoubtedly terrify the hip boomer, even though this is apparently a song about forsaking vice for a life of gospel rectitude. I don't know if it will make much headway in the fiercely competitive and novelty-hungry world of commercial rap, though. One of the problems with a lot of Christian music is that it waits for a trend in popular music to be codified, and then copies it. But by then, most fans have moved on to new variations. On the other hand, this song—done in a popular style of rap called "crunk"— politely asks the listener whether she's wondered why human beings are prone to doing "things Elohim really isn't fond of." When's the last time anyone on *American Idol* sang a song with the word *Elohim* in it?

TRACK 5: "Annihilate the Corrupt" by Demon Hunter. I really have no idea what I'm listening to here. It's Christian metal, a genre I wanted to check out just to make sure it exists. I guess it sounds enough like metal:

grinding guitars, bass drums played at ludicrous speed, a singer with a voice like a wolverine gargling gravel. I'm not sure what the lyrics are about; the only words I can make out are "I am the face of your affliction," which suggest this will not be a popular selection at senior prom spotlight dances. But boy, you'd be amazed to find out there are hundreds of Christian metal bands, often with names that sound intimidating only if you don't know what they mean: there are bands called Ekklesia, Pantokrator, and—wonderfully—Maximum Pentecost. Historically in Christianity there have been arguments that some types of music are well-suited for sacred songs, while others are not. The Catholic Church, for example, was briefly suspicious of polyphony, while the Orthodox still don't play any instruments during the Divine Liturgy. For my part, I think I draw the line somewhere prior to Christian metal. At some point, arguably, the form overwhelms the content, like at an especially tacky wedding.

ROCKING WITH JESUS
A COMPLICATED FUTURE

As you can see, contemporary Christian rock gets mixed results. On the one hand, the music is nothing like the bland, Sunday school fare pictured by detractors (particularly not Interment At Golgotha). On the other, it often fails in its bid to do two things at once. Either the message overwhelms the music, which comes off as stale or compromised, or the musical style drowns out any attempt to express sentiments other than the sort of lyrical banalities familiar to mainstream music.

The Internet Theologian's various trips to Christian rock festivals underscored this split personality phenomenon. At first blush, there was nothing to distinguish these concerts from their secular counterparts: they were vast fields full of young people milling around, discussing their body piercings, and paying seven dollars for a hamburger. Loud music came from stages around the festival, and bands sold T-shirts and concert merchandise.

The differences emerged only when you looked closer: the information booths weren't demanding the liberation of Tibet or the legalization of marijuana, they were urging people to declare Jesus their personal savior. And the skaters performing tricks on the demonstration half pipes wore T-shirts that said "Praise Him" rather than, say, "Adidas."

Above all, the festivals revealed the absence of contradiction, the kind of creative tension one might expect from the meeting of two worldviews that are—theoretically, anyway—hostile, if not completely incompatible. As I watched concertgoers line up in front of the Temporary Tattoo Tent to get "3:16" emblazoned on their forearms, I thought, *We've come a long way from Jerry Lee Lewis, who gargled fistfuls of pills to blot out the guilt he felt at turning his back on God to play rock and roll music.*

And then, it struck me: a Frisbee, thrown by careless teens, right between my eyes. After the teens helped me to my feet, I decided to engage them about the music they loved and why it seemed so weird to outsiders.

I'll call the first teen Mandy, because that's her name. She's sixteen years old and attends a small public high school. She wants to go to college and eventually be an oceanographer.[15] She's saving herself for marriage, her favorite band is A Distant Star, and she accepted Jesus as her savior when she was thirteen years old.

---

[15] Oceanography is the study of singer Billy Ocean.

Mandy does not see much contradiction between the faith she embraces and the music and culture in which she participates.

"As long as we're not doing things that are going to hurt us, I don't see what the problem is," she said. "There's nothing wrong with serving the Lord and having fun with your friends."

Mandy's friend—whom I'll call Justin even though his name is Todd—agreed.

"I think it's stupid to say there's something wrong with this music, period," Justin said. "It's not what they're playing, it's why they're playing and what they're singing about. Even if it doesn't seem to other people like they're really expressing a Christian message, they're not putting out something negative, either."

Justin is also sixteen and, like Mandy, plans to go to college, but not to write books about the singer of "Caribbean Queen." Instead, he wants get a teaching degree and teach math in inner city schools.

After the kids ran off with their Frisbee, I walked to the concession tent and munched thoughtfully on a six dollar hot dog.[16] Perhaps my hard labors as an Internet Theologian had preoccupied me with purely theoretical considerations, leaving the "real world" experience of people like Mandy and Justin out of the equation. Perhaps that sort of concrete application was what I was missing from my comprehensive, in-depth look at Christian music.

What surprised me most about Mandy and Justin was that they were both so obviously well-adjusted. When the Internet Theologian was sixteen, he was a depressed,

---

[16] Which I also plan to write off, and which absolutely is a business expense.

misanthropic mess, scorning the world and spending his time plotting for the day when he would return to the high school reunion as a famous author and heap scorn on all of those who had crossed him in his adolescent days. What's more, this description is true of virtually everyone in my high school, including the guidance counselors. Especially them, come to think of it.

At any rate, music for me was largely an expression of my discontent with everything as it then existed, and my research tells me most secular critics and fans hold similar conceptions of music. And, in a way, perhaps that's what fans of sacred music believed all those years ago, at the dawn of the rock and roll era: that music was a means to convey their deepest hopes and anxieties and shouldn't be trivialized by the passing fancies of the marketplace.

Mandy and Justin are from a different generation, however—one not as marinated in angst as its forebears. Maybe it's the consciously Christian upbringing; maybe it's the startling advances in behavior-modifying prescription medication in the last ten years. Whatever the case, there are now millions of young Americans for whom the contradictions between sacred meaning and secular pleasure are relics of history.

And perhaps it was always meant to be that way. After all, as St. Paul says in his epistle to the Liverpudlians: "I know it's only rock and roll. But I like it."[17]

---

[17] Admittedly, this is coming from the apocryphal Gospel of Ringo, which scholars have called into question by noting the presence of anachronistic terms like "howdy-do, pardner," "snafu," and "candlepin bowling."

A FIELD GUIDE TO THE MAJOR
NORTH AMERICAN JESUSES

Many years ago, a very wise man[1] observed: "God created man in His image, and man has been returning the favor ever since." This is especially true of Jesus which, when you think about it, is sort of counterintuitive.

After all, it's God the Father who seems to lend himself best to creative misinterpretation. In the book of Genesis, G the F even refers to himself by two different names: the singular YHWH and the plural Elohim. He (they?) even says, "Let us make man in our own image," which has divided scholars ever since: Is Genesis hinting at an early polytheism among the Hebrew nation? Or is God using the royal "we" as part of a Queen Victoria impression?

At any rate, this multiple name phenomenon seems like it could have led to a host of arguments about precisely who God the Father is. Given the violent history of religion, it's remarkable that there weren't a series of bloody wars over whether God's name is "Elohim" or "YHWH."

---

[1] It was "Stone Cold" Steve Austin.

The ruffle-collared, buckle-hatted Englishmen who produced the Bible translation eventually known as the King James Version even got into the spirit, whimsically deciding that God the Father should be called "Jehovah," even though that's a completely made-up, phony baloney name with no Hebrew equivalent.

The fun ends there, though, as far as Elohim/YHWH/Jehovah is concerned. But it never stops when it comes to Jesus.

In fact, there seem to be more Jesuses every year, with the creation of new Sons of Man standing as a virtual growth industry. Economists now estimate that the manufacture of new Jesuses is responsible for about eleven percent of the United States's gross domestic product. Without resorting to hyperbole, then, if we stopped coming up with new versions of Jesus, our economy would go into a tailspin, grass would grow in the streets, the living would envy the dead, and basic cable packages would be scaled back to two networks and a community announcements channel in Spanish.

It's a little strange there should be so much disagreement on who Jesus is, was, or will be. After all, Jesus—unlike God the Father, say, or Johnny Appleseed—was a real human being with a real historical existence. Arguing over who he "really" was seems a little like arguing over whether Franklin Roosevelt could fly (for the record: he could, but not very well).

"Come now," you object. "Unlike Franklin Roosevelt—who was president as recently as the Wars of Spanish Succession—Jesus lived long, long ago in a galaxy far, far away. It's only natural that there should be disagreement and dissension over such a distant figure."

To which the Internet Theologian replies: you're

right, *except* for the parts about which you're dead wrong. Disagreement over the person of Jesus has been with us almost as long as the Christian religion. This suggests, perhaps, that Christians will never be able to agree on *anything*, but I digress.

DEBATES OVER JESUS
THE FOURTH CENTURY'S VERSION OF SUDOKU

The Internet Theologian begins this discussion by boldly setting aside the controversy over Jesus among Jews in the Holy Land[2] that erupted after the crucifixion. This is because the Internet Theologian found no user-friendly Web sites about this historical controversy; thus, we can infer it's a minor matter. It is, though, worth noting that in the early decades of the first century there were already at least two Jesuses: the resurrected Son of God and the scorned criminal heretic. This disagreement would turn out to be a portent of things to come.

The real fight over Jesus began sometime in the second half of the first century, which seems awfully early. Indeed, even if all the original Apostles had been beheaded, crucified upside down, stoned to death, sawed in half, and gunned down in Acutane-related freakouts by then, there were still plenty of people who "shook the hand that shook the hand," so to speak.

There was, for example, St. Polycarp of Smyrna, who as a young man probably knew St. John the Evangelist, who as a young man knew Jesus (who, as a young man, *was* Jesus). People like Polycarp must have been awfully confused by early Christian heretics like the Doceticists,

---

[2] Waterbury, Conn.

who insisted that Jesus was a sort of ghost who only *seemed* to have lived on earth. Arguments with these people must have been deeply frustrating.

"But I knew John the Evangelist, who knew Jesus personally," Polycarp would say in exasperation.

"No," the Doceticists would patiently explain. "John knew Ghost Jesus, the Imaginary Man. You see, it's all very simple."

Of course it wasn't simple; nothing was simple in the era before the World Wide Web enabled us to check cited sources within seconds. Back then, orthodox Christians probably had to trudge to the library to refute the heretics, and that could take days, especially if other theologians had checked out the books beforehand. Do you have any idea how slow interlibrary loans were in the first century? Frankly, it was easier just to excommunicate people.

Anyway, the followers of Docetism (from the Latin *docetus*; literally, "arguing like a moron") soon disappeared, and the stage was set for centuries of much more complex and genuinely tiresome debate over the nature of Jesus.

Before long, everyone like Polycarp who had met someone who met Jesus was killed in a variety of gruesome and horrific ways that even today make us wonder if the Roman Empire would have lasted longer if they had devoted less ingenuity to capital punishment and more to building walls to stop the Vandals from getting in.

However, the death of friends of eyewitnesses meant that Jesus Creation was able to spread like a theological wildfire. This wildfire burst forth in the controlled burn of Arianism, which was only extinguished by the airdrop of orthodoxy, assisted ironically by the forest clearcutting of Julian the Apostate.

The Arians were, naturally, followers of Arius, a

priest who spent his time putting new words to popular sea chanteys. At some point, he decided that, while Jesus was pretty super, he wasn't quite as super as his Father. In fact, Jesus wasn't even of the same basic stuff as God the Father—although, to be sure, Jesus was one super dude.

This caused a great deal of consternation among the orthodox, who, to make matters worse, also hated sea chanteys. Arius was, additionally, such an unpleasant character that he got punched out by Santa Claus at the Council of Nicea.[3]

Arius eventually died in a bizarre bathroom accident, and really, the matter should have ended there. Who'd want to be a member of the party of the guy who exploded outside an outhouse? But the ancient world being what it was, debate over Jesus went on and on. It's from these sharp theological controversies over Christology that we get the term "one iota," meaning a miniscule point that pointy-headed nerds will argue about until they pass out from low blood sugar.

The argument, which lasted more than fifty years, hinged over whether Christ could be described as *homoousious*, "of the same substance" as God, or whether it was not much more obviously correct to describe Jesus as *homoiousious*, "of a similar substance." You'll be relieved to know that eventually they decided Christ could be no other than *homoousious*, but scholars are unanimous today in determining the fourth century to be an exceptionally boring time to be alive, if this argument was any indication.

These debates are as alien to our twenty-first century minds as the concept of subtle standup comedy. Why?

---

[3] True! Sort of. Look it up.

Because, in modern times, we've learned a tremendously important lesson that would have cut the Council of Ephesus down to approval of the previous meeting's minutes and "other business" before adjournment. That lesson is: if you don't like the Jesus you're faced with, you can always make up your own.

This brings us, with all the swift logic of a nightmare, to our field guide. This is not intended to be the definitive compendium of all Jesuses; the Internet Theologian has neither the space nor the willingness to wade through hundreds of church groups' clumsily built Web pages to create such a document.

However, I have here prepared a series of thumbnail profiles meant as a decent introduction to some of the major Jesuses of the North American continent: who they are, what they want, and what to do if they show up at your apartment asking to use your phone. And, just maybe, it will include helpful hints you can use when making up your own Jesus. So, without further ado, let's look at those Lords!

EXTREME JESUS

Also known as:
The Son of Gnarly, Jesus is My Homeboy, Tattoo Jesus, Skateboard Jesus, the Surprisingly-Conservative-Considering-All-the-Piercings-Christ.

Distinguishing characteristics:
Carefully sculpted facial hair, tasteful tattoos, love of rap music, ability to "shred a half pipe," familiarity with surfing lingo, frighteningly *au courant*.

Habitat:
Skate parks, warehouse spaces turned into churches, hip neighborhoods from Austin to Seattle, cross-country "faith tours," bestselling DVDs featuring skateboarders hugging and talking about "living for Him."

Description: Listen up: this ain't your father's Jesus. If you're old enough to remember the Carter administration, it likely isn't your Jesus, either. In fact, if anyone in your family seems to gravitate toward Extreme Jesus, it's your weird younger brother, who always seems to be wearing shorts no matter how cold it is outside, and whose musical taste runs from deafening rap music to deafening rock music.

THE WORD

That's right; this is a Jesus for the critical sixteen to twenty-five demographic, which nowadays includes people in their late twenties and thirties who just wish they were still part of that demographic. Extreme Jesus is routinely described as "edgy," as an "outsider" not afraid to "shake things up." That their theology casts the Divine Logos essentially as an unruly occupant of detention hall does not deter the advocates of Extreme Jesus. In fact, this brand is one of the leading Jesuses on the market, vastly outperforming that old 1970s standby, Groovy Jesus.

Extreme Jesus is most frequently encountered in hip churches with blown-glass fixtures instead of stained glass windows and in books with titles like *No Tolerance For Sissy Church*. These are outlets for Extreme Jesus to express the two eternal verities of the Christian religion: absolute biblical literalism and motocross.

The pointyheaded theo-nerd reading this will probably object at this point that there is extremely little motocross actually depicted in the Bible,[4] but—as the Internet Theologian tirelessly shows—trivial arguments like this one are why people don't like pointyheaded theo-nerds. Extreme Jesus isn't afraid of contradictions: he thinks people can be faithful to the original principles of the Apostolic church *and* ride bitchin' motor scooters to punk rock Sunday school; he thinks women should quit their jobs to stay home with the kids *and* have neck tattoos!

---

[4] Just a few scattered references in Acts, really.

If you're wondering whether you're ready to hang with Extreme Jesus, ask yourself a few questions:

Have you recently attended a multimedia sermon punctuated by shredding guitar solos and inexplicable pictures of rappers wearing fur coats?

Have you ever slammed down a double-tall espresso, hopped on your Vespa, and driven like a wildebeest in pursuit of a gazelle just to get to an Xtreme Street Luge/ Pray-In?

Do you think God possibly had anything to do with the 1996 Pauly Shore vehicle *Bio-Dome*?

Does it seem feasible to describe the Godhead, the unknowable Triune Lord who is Three-Yet-One, as "eff-ing sweet"?

If you answered "yes" or "no" to any of these questions, then I'm sorry: you're clearly not cut out for Extreme Jesus. Why don't you shuffle off to your safe, nine to five Jesus and enjoy some sports that don't involve crashing into walls while wearing shin pads? Sellout.

To those who, rather than answering verbally, simply contorted your fingers into the "hang 10" gesture and bellowed: you have already been initiated into the profound mysteries of Extreme Jesus. Welcome aboard, fellow "gnarpostles" (gnarly apostles).

CHRIST AMONG THE NPR LISTENERS

Also known as:
Feelin' Groovy Jesus, Whole Foods Jesus, Prius Christ, the Alpha, the Omega, and All the Socially Disadvantaged Letters in Between.

Distinguishing characteristics:
Ponytail, jeans with sports jacket, headband, ability to turn water into pricey Pinot Noir, fondness for the cinema of Robert Altman, subscription to *The Nation*.

Habitat:
Coffee shops that only stock organically grown, fair trade brews harvested by farmers making a living wage (or, in a pinch, Starbucks); Unitarian Universalist meeting houses (but only for the community art show); among the downtrodden and the Peace Studies majors.

Description: Looking for Christ among the NPR Listeners? Well, I've got news for you, Mr. Fundamentalist Fire-and-Brimstone Moral Majority: you're looking in the wrong place. Because you won't find Whole Foods Jesus in *church*, unless there's a same-sex commitment ceremony going on, or possibly a blessing somehow involving house pets.

THE WORD

This Jesus doesn't care a wit for all those pay-pray-obey types who give Christians a bad name. This Jesus said "Judge not lest ye be judged," and not much else; something about Reagan, maybe, and how he was bad.

At any rate, this is the Jesus worshiped (or at least acknowledged) by people who festoon their hybrid cars with bumper stickers proclaiming their opposition to everything from hate to the current lineup of CNN's "Capital Gang."

This is not the kind of Jesus who lays a guilt trip on you for committing adultery or dealing a little pot or passing military secrets to the North Vietnamese during the 1960s. No, indeed: if this Jesus could have added anything to the Beatitudes, it would be "blessed are the open-minded, for they shall inherit the beautiful three-bedroom co-op overlooking the park."

This Jesus doesn't care about your sex life or whom you vote for or whether you worship other gods or anything else you might do, although he is a little concerned that your current automobile isn't quite as fuel-efficient as it could be.

After all, in the Bible, Jesus was more concerned with feeding the hungry, clothing the naked, and visiting the prisoners, wasn't he? Of course, not all of these apply today, and we shouldn't make the mistake of taking Jesus too literally.

We shouldn't just assume that naked people want clothes; they may be expressing their human right to be nude. And, ugh, have you ever been to a prison or, more likely, seen the one on *Oz*? Probably in Jesus' time, prisons were more pastoral, with more time for crafts and things like that.

So, forget the naked thing and the prisons. That leaves us with feeding the hungry, which is certainly noble, but isn't that the government's job?

But, anyway, don't worry if you can't get around to all that stuff, or *any* of that stuff. As it says in the Bible, "It's the thought that counts."[5]

In fact, Christ among the NPR Listeners is such a laid-back, nonjudgmental guy that it's pretty hard to imagine why the Romans executed him by nailing him to a cross after torturing him. Perhaps *they* were the religious fundamentalists of their day and Jesus enraged them by suggesting that women had larger roles to play in the imperial cult than just being vestal virgins; it's not entirely clear.

Although this Jesus may seem extremely watery and vague in what he wants, he is one of the most popular of the North American Sons of Man.

---

[5] It's in the Book of Adlai, chapter 3, verse 4.

PRESIDENT JESUS

Also known as:
Stump Speech Jesus, the Suffering Spaghetti Dinner Attendee, On-Message Jesus, the Christ of the Push Polls.

Distinguishing characteristics:
Suit and tie (rolled-up sleeves when visiting with the common folk), PDA, dazzling smile that stays in place even in the face of crying babies and yammering Pharisees, promises promises promises.

Habitat:
The campaign trail, the halls of power, the precinct, the polling place, and the strategically placed letter to the editor.

Description: As Jesus said to the Apostles, "What good is this teaching, but that you use it to build a veto-proof majority?"[6] Well, maybe not the Jesus you're familiar with, but President Jesus certainly said it.

[6] Admittedly a rather "free" translation of Mark 2:11.

THE WORD

Of course, Jesus did say "My Father's kingdom is not of this world," and that's all very well and good: monarchies test poorly among focus groups these days. But notice that Jesus never said, "My Father's *bicameral legislature* is not of this world." As St. Augustine noted, anything not expressly forbidden by the Bible is permitted,[7] and therefore Christians have a commission to go forth and spread the good news about President Jesus.

Don't think for a second that your concerns about property taxes, zoning regulations, and saucy Super Bowl halftime shows aren't important to President Jesus. As Jesus himself noted, he counts even the hairs on your head, so he's got to know how ridiculous your mill rate is becoming, what with these morons on the city council.

President Jesus, in other words, wants to be more than merely the savior of all mankind: he wants to be the guy who helps determine what the sales tax should be.

An example drawn from the Gospel of Luke[8] helps shed light on President Jesus:

President Jesus and his cabinet of apostles were walking to some township or other outside of Jerusalem — Galilee, Galileo, Ceasarea Salad Philippi, the location name

---

[7] He never actually said anything remotely like this.

[8] Again, this anecdote is only "in" the Gospel of Luke in the sense that Godot is "in" *Waiting for Godot*: You could say it exists even more fully in absence than it does if it were present. You could also say I just made it up to illustrate a stupid point. Both are valid.

doesn't really matter. The point is: they were approached by a young man who had a question. Jesus seemed to be approached by people with questions all the time in the Bible. You have to wonder what kind of society it was if everyone turned to roaming carpenters for advice.

At any rate, this young man (let's call him Karl) approached President Jesus and the cabinet and asked of him, "Lord—tell me, is it moral for me to promote my chosen candidate by smearing his opponent with any useful libel that comes to hand? What if his opponent is a real sissy, Lord? I mean a genuine Yale-bred, white-glove, Grade A poodle?"

To which President Jesus replied, "Sell all that you own and give it to the pollsters. And good ones, too. Forget the polls taken by computers dialing telephones; that's about as scientific as cold fusion."

And the people were greatly troubled by these sayings.

JESUS H. BUDDHA

Also known as:
Allah,
Krishna,
Siddhartha,
Ahura Mazda,
L. Ron,
Clapton, etc.

Distinguishing characteristics:
Appears however you choose to perceive him. (Alas, this approach does not work for blind dates.)

Habitat:
Anywhere there are men and women whose hearts yearn for the transcendent, usually in the New Age and Metaphysics section of larger chain bookstores.

Description: We live in "post-precise" times. The days when a bunch of Syrian bishops with unpronounceable names sat down and argued bitterly about whether we can really call Mary the Mother of God are over. Today, we prefer a God as adaptable and flexible as a good mountain bike; a God that suits our passing interests in Eastern philosophy, the mystery religions, or professional hockey. A God, in other words, like Jesus H. Buddha.

THE WORD

The most important thing to remember about JHB is that he is all things to all men, and most things to a vast majority of women. So the person known to modern Westerners as "Jesus" was also called "Quetzalcoatl" by the ancient Aztecs, "Gautama" by the people of India, and "Josh" by his friends growing up in Nazareth.

After all, virtually all religions teach the same thing, but in different terms.[9] Instead of believing that one religion is "right" and others "wrong," it's much more logical to agree that all contain "rightness" in equal measure; besides that, such diplomacy cuts down on the chance of getting punched in the nose.

For example, let's look at these side-by-side comparisons of the teachings of Jesus and Buddha:

1 BUDDHA: Taught there was no God.
JESUS: Taught that he was God, as well as the Son of God.

2 BUDDHA: Believed all existence was suffering.
JESUS: Believed all existence was a blessing from the Creator.

3 BUDDHA: Warned that souls will be reincarnated until they reach a state of enlightenment.
JESUS: Warned that all souls will be judged immediately after death and can only be saved by God's grace.

There, you see? Virtually identical!

When you look at them that way, it's easy to see why

---

[9] Except Zoroastrianism. What a misbegotten freak show that is.

so many credulous hippies believe Jesus actually traveled to India to learn from Buddhist monks. The idea is really plausible, except for the fact that flights to India from the Jerusalem airport back then were notoriously overbooked.

Now, a number of religious types will probably choose this moment to object that, in fact, there are some key differences between most religions. In a very narrow, Western sense, I suppose it is true that, for example, in Islam and Judaism the concept of God having a human son who was also God is somewhat problematic. And there is the very minor point that adherents to many religions have shown themselves frequently willing either to suffer or inflict extraordinary harm to safeguard their particular interpretation of theology. But that just goes to show you how wretched the world was before the invention of Comparative Religions courses: people simply didn't know how much they had in common until an academic who doesn't believe in God at all clued them in. And even after completing their formal study, they weren't able to comprehend fully their similarities until the Internet Theologian was able to sum things up succinctly in a comment box post on Beliefnet.

Now we know better. If the great works of world literature—the Bible, the Koran, the Bhagavad-Gita, the Book of Mormon, the Star Wars novelizations, and *My Prison Without Bars* by Pete Rose—can all be summed up in a single phrase, that phrase would be: "Be nice to people." And, in the case of Pete Rose's book, it would also be: "Don't bet on baseball."

BIG BANK JESUS

Also known as:

Lord Vegas,
Prosperity Jesus, Jesus
"Take Up Your Cross, but
Now That You Mention It,
a Cross of Gold Would
Probably Be Extremely
Lucrative in Today's Market" Christ,
the Price is Jesus!

Distinguishing characteristics:

Tan,
manicure,
expensive sandals,
resolutely upbeat attitude about
life,
aversion to the poor.

Habitat:

Suburban megachurches,
seminars by former CEOs
who explain how the Book
of Job helped them get the
most from their investments,
Cadillac dealerships.

Description:
Although Christians don't like to admit it, their religion has historically suffered because of its attraction to losers. Everywhere you find a Christian church, you're likely to find a bunch of whining pity-me-Charlies, their calloused mitts reaching in expectation of another handout.

The Word

Take India for example. The world's largest religious marketplace, and when Christianity makes it over there, who do they sign up in record numbers? The aristocratic Brahmins? The macho warrior caste? The humble but productive merchants? No—the Untouchables! And not the good, Elliot Ness-Kevin Costner-Al Capone kind! People who were such absolute zeroes that no one wanted to touch them!

This image of Christianity as a theological cot shelter is deceptive, though. And no one knows that better than Big Bank Jesus.

Big Bank Jesus is at the heart of a movement called "prosperity theology," which essentially goes like this: God wants you to be happy. It would be nice if you were the kind of person who could be happy with a beautiful sunset or a day spent washing old people at the hospital, but that's just not the way it is. You're happy with money. More specifically, you're happy with the kind of money that allows you to have expanded digital cable just so you can watch ESPN in Spanish to hear if it sounds funny. And so God hooks you up with all the cash you want. In exchange, you thank God and consider sponsoring a litter pickup on the Interstate on behalf of your church.

After centuries of losing high-rolling society types because of all that "preferential option for the poor" jive, Big Bank Jesus is finally bringing Christianity to the kind of people who wouldn't look out of place in a beach house at the Hamptons.

And before you start carping about how this is all the product of some sinister American love of luxury, just save it.

My exhaustive Internet theological researches have demonstrated that they love Big Bank Jesus in what used to be known as the Third World, too. In the Philippines, for example, one branch of the Big Bank Jesus movement demonstrates its enthusiasm for wealth by having its members turn open umbrellas upwards to the sky in a gesture symbolic of their desire to capture the wealth streaming from heaven. Granted, this is both distressingly literalistic and, in a rainy climate, a poor use of umbrellas, but still, the point is, they like money. And what's wrong with that?

Okay, so there are some minor, obscure passages in the Bible regarding certain undesirable side effects of wealth. Jesus at one point does say something about it being easier for a camel to go through the eye of the needle than for a rich man to enter the Kingdom of Heaven, but what most people miss is that Jesus was *kidding*. The Bible, in fact, is full of puns, laugh lines, and zingers, and this one is illustrative of Our Lord's trademark zany absurdism. I mean, a camel going through the eye of a needle? That's pretty hilarious!

And, yes, there is "The Epistle of James," which says something like: "Howl and weep, ye rich, you have heaped up treasures in the last days," blah blah blah. But this James was a completely insignificant figure in the early church,[10] comparable in importance to those Ameri-

---

[10] St. James the Just, first bishop of Jerusalem and, according to St. Paul, "brother of the Lord" (Galatians 1:19) and one of the three pillars of the Church (2:9). Feast day: May 3.

can presidents from the late nineteenth century who no one can remember who they are. It's clear that his epistle was included largely to pad out the Letters section of the Bible, which editors felt was being hogged by Paul.

POP HISTORICAL JESUS

Also known as:
Yeshua ben Yosiah,
a Humble Carpenter,
the Accidental Messiah,
Seminar Jesus.

Distinguishing characteristics:
Tight-lipped about his own good qualities, humble, nondescript, in no way causing the sort of trouble that you would imagine would precipitate a crucifixion.

Habitat:
Thick, unread monographs with titles like "Parsing the Peacemakers: The Sermon On the Mount Reconsidered in a Postmodern Context," media-friendly conferences hosted by gregarious ex-clergymen, myths.

Description: As the undivided Christian Church determined at the Council of Narnia,[11] Jesus is both fully man and fully God. This leads to a number of metaphysical problems, not least of which is whether you have to get him two birthday presents. And what do you get for someone who's fully God, anyway? Should you even bother wrapping it? I mean, he already knows what it is.

---

[11] c. 383. Among other decisions, the council agreed on the use of that fish logo for bumper stickers.

THE WORD

To avoid headaches such as this altogether, an exciting new movement in pseudohistory has revised the decisions of the Council and simply set aside the "fully God" portion of Jesus. In place of the "Jesus of Faith," they're pledged to examine the "Jesus of History," the man behind the myth, the human element at the heart of the Greatest Story Ever Told.

Of course, it's virtually impossible to do that, because we know almost nothing about Jesus.

Historical records from the first century are generally poor, even for famous people. Take the Greek playwright Agathon, who lived in the fifth century B.C. One of the most famous men of his day, all that remains for us are two fragments (one of which, in the supremely bitchy irony of which history is fond, is "Even the gods can't change history") and his portrayal in Plato's *Symposium*, which paints Agathon as something of a priss.

If we know nothing about Agathon other than that he couldn't hold his wine, what can we know about an obscure carpenter from a backwater of the Roman Empire who was put to death for causing a civil disturbance?

Apart from the New Testament and a few stray mentions in the work of first-century Jewish historian Josephus, there's not much to go on. You'd think this would stop pop Historical Jesus scholars in their tracks. You, apparently, have never been to college.

In the absence of documentary evidence, these scholars rely on what Arnold Toynbee called "an historian's great friends: conjecture, rumor, hyperbole, and bold invention."[12]

In their top secret labs, these scholars have produced a number of theories about Jesus, many of which have gained credibility on that great conveyer of authenticity: the Internet. Here is a small sampling of these subsets of Jesuses:

1 JESUS THE POLITICAL REVOLUTIONARY: According to this thesis, Jesus wanted nothing to do with an other-worldly Kingdom of God but wanted instead to establish something very like the Cambridge City Council in Jerusalem. The evidence for this is conjecture about other messianic movements coupled with wishful thinking.

2 JESUS THE SILENT TYPE: This line of thinking holds that most of what is attributed to Jesus in the Bible is nothing more than fanciful nonsense created by later hagiographers. This is richly ironic given that the New Testament was written within a century of Jesus' death, whereas the contemporary scholars are writing 1,970 years or so afterward, but put aside your facile notions about "plausibility." Jesus can't be known by historical record but by using a series of colored balls to determine what he really said![13] The most reliable tool for determining what Jesus really said, according to this view, is whether the message in question sounds like something you agree with. So whereas I

---

[12] Of course he never said anything like that. At least, as far as I know. Confession: I have never read a word of Arnold Toynbee.

[13] This is actually done at one well-publicized gathering of Pop Scholars. Before you sneer, recall that the Constitution and Bill of Rights were written in similar fashion.

find it unlikely that Jesus said, "I come not to bring peace, but a sword," I find convincing evidence for his having said, "The only thing more annoying than the New York Yankees is their fanbase."

3 JESUS, THE PROTAGONIST OF LOST BOOKS: A key document used by these scholars is the so-called "Q" document, so named because it was thought up during a particularly intense session of Q-Bert on the old Colecovision back in 1984. Q consists of nothing more than sayings attributed to Jesus and provides a valuable insight into what Christ *really* said and believed before layers of interpretation and interpolation were added on by later commentators. The only problem with this elegant thesis is that the Q document is purely imaginary; that is, it *doesn't* exist, but scholars agree it would be great if it *did* exist, much like a good bar that's cheap and unpretentious but that doesn't have terrible bands playing on the weekends. The difference here is that if you pretend that such a bar exists, you'll have nowhere to go on Friday night, but if you pretend the Q document exists, you could get tenure.

4 THE JESUS WHO WASN'T THERE: A school of thought popular with cranks on the Internet holds that Jesus didn't actually exist. Citing a lack of documentary evidence apart from the New Testament, Josephus, and Roman records,[14] the adherents of this thesis argue that Jesus was a canny invention by either (a) St. Paul, (b) Josephus, (c) a Roman aristocratic

---

[14] One wonders what would suffice as proof. A signed credit card statement? A Galilee High School Senior Yearbook, class of 18 A.D.?

family, or (d) shadowy New Orleans businessman Clay Shaw. Bless their hearts, but it's hard not suspect them of having motives that are not entirely historical in nature, especially when you consider that they don't seem to spend much time arguing about the historical veracity of Moses, Zarathustra, Buddha, or the fourteen U.S. presidents who came before George Washington.

All of the above, of course, represent only the smallest smattering of the North American Jesuses. If the Internet Theologian were so inclined—and if, more importantly, he could find a way to use it as a tax deduction—he could spend months cataloguing every different type of Jesus at large in our republic.

In virtually every corner of this great continent—not to mention the other, lesser continents abroad—you can find a new version of Jesus wherever you find a group of people with an obscure gripe and a desire for attention.

Maybe one Jesus is a little more interested in social justice than another; maybe a Southern-fried Jesus is a bit folksier than his Northeastern counterpart. In some truly alarming instances, you will find people claiming not only that their version of Jesus is present here on earth, but that he's asking you to fork over your life savings in order to live with him on a compound behind barbed wire.

Truly, the confusion of messiahs must gladden the heart of Jesus, whoever he is/was/will be, for didn't he say: "Wherever two or more gathered, they will be unable to agree on even the most basic facts about me?"[15]

---

[15] No; he didn't.

A WAY, THE TRUTHINESS, AND THE LIFESTYLE

It's Sunday morning in America.

From the wave-battered Atlantic coastline to the majesty of the Sierra Madres, in the little storefront churches of the South and in the whitewashed Lutheran chapels of the plains states, Americans are at prayer. Whether they worship in traditional ways or utilize the latest in cutting-edge technology to augment their prayer, they have all assembled in common fellowship to acknowledge the glory of God.

Their faith—manifest in reading the Scriptures, in participating in the sacraments, in the bonds of joining together for communal prayer—is a powerful testament to the durability of what began nearly twenty centuries ago in a far-flung backwater of the Roman Empire, and what has come to define the American people as a spiritual nation.

It is also a testament, of course, to the cluelessness of the schmucks.

I mean, the whole point of Christianity isn't sitting

around in some "church" and "praying" to a distant "God": it's to complain bitterly about the current government at a local community arts show. Am I right?

That, anyway, is the contention of a large but mostly unnoticed branch of Christianity, the Christians for whom Jesus, Gandhi, the Dalai Lama, Martin Luther King Jr., and Robert Mapplethorpe basically had the same message: *hope you're feelin' groovy, friend.*

We touched upon this overlooked segment of Christianity in our previous chapter. You'll no doubt recall how we earlier demonstrated that the preferred deity of this group is Christ among the NPR Listeners. But while the taxonomy of this important subculture is crystal clear to a trained observer like the Internet Theologian, it somehow escapes the notice of the so-called "pundits" and "experts" on American religion, who are perhaps too busy collecting giant speaking fees and holding forth on cable news shows to recognize the sins.

Allow me.

The first thing to know about this subculture is that it primarily flourishes in coastal areas and suburbs. These are welcoming havens for people who are sure that the core of Jesus' teaching relates to hybrid cars.

These folks are often given the misleading sobriquet "liberal Christians." We will not use such nomenclature here, in an effort to discourage the thoughtless mixing of theology and ideology.

Indeed, one of the great burdens the Internet Theologian must bear is the nearly universal habit of bringing the terms of political discourse to bear on the wholly different universe of religion. This is largely due to the influence of the Internet Theologian's ill-mannered cousin, the Internet Political Scientist, and also partly to the fact that

Americans just can't get enough of shouting at each other about politics. Americans, if you let them, will see politics in *everything*: religion, education, health, dessert menus, and the career trajectory of Mickey Rourke. But just as not all things go well with peanut butter, not all subjects can be illuminated by recourse to political jargon.

Take "liberal" and "conservative," terms familiar to virtually all Americans who are not Amish. There is great temptation to apply these to every aspect of human life, so as to make things more comprehensible; it's a definite possibility that more Americans would watch the World Cup if soccer could somehow be reduced to one of these two words.

An American who opposes the death penalty, for example, is likely to be "liberal," while someone who opposes abortion is likely to be "conservative." But many Christians are able to hold these opinions simultaneously and claim that doing so is not a contradiction. This raises the possibility either that these Christians are fibbing, or that commonplace political terms don't really capture the complexities of human beliefs—and that fact is particularly troublesome if we attempt to impose political labels on theological convictions.

To describe the American religious landscape accurately, therefore, the Internet Theologian cannot rely on the lazy shorthand of the political realm. He must bear down into the heart of the complex theological issues and use his judicious wealth of knowledge to create the perfect term, one that will serve as both an explanatory label for nonspecialists and an accurate reflection of that which is being described.

With that in mind, I have named this particular group "Grown-Up Hippie Christians."

Why? Well, let's look at the facts. Most of these Christians are adults—in fact, most are approaching the age at which they are referred to by politicians as "cherished older Americans." The average median age of their group tends to be indicated by their ability to explain correctly what a Packard was.[1]

But, while they may be old enough to remember Dick Clark for something other than counting down from ten on December 31, they were honest-to-goodness hippies when they were young and have retained residual sympathies for all things groovy. Make no mistake: they are not hippies today. They have good jobs and retirements, sensible four-door sedans, and tastefully decorated homes in the suburbs. At heart, though, they're still doing that cosmic noodle dance that hippies do while teaching the world to sing.

Grown-Up Hippie Christians are important for our purposes because they have such a close and familiar relationship with popular culture. Since childhood, when TV was invented by Milton Berle, these people have thought of their lives in terms of popular culture, from the Beatles to the satisfying documentaries of the Sundance Channel.

And just as no one is better suited to explain Christianity than the Internet Theologian, no group is more skilled than the Grown-Up Hippie Christians at translating the confusing world of theology to the argot of pop culture. So why don't they get more attention?

As mentioned above, Grown-Up Hippie Christians—or GUHCs, for short—have largely been forgotten in discussions of the American religious scene. When pundits turn to Christianity, they turn to the broad mass of

---

[1] It was a dog that got Vice President Nixon into trouble.

evangelical Protestants (generally believed to be "conservative") and even to small, obscure sects like the Roman Catholics (generally believed to be European).

Discussions of American Christianity, then, tend to take for granted the "facts" that most Christians belong to a "low church"[2] denomination like the Baptists or whatever those ones on Sunday morning church TV shows are; that most Christians believe in the gift of tongues or "glossolalia"[3] and other such "charisms of the (Holy) Spirit"; and that Christians are likely to vote Republican, own a pickup truck, and regard most contemporary art with disfavor.

Such crude stereotypes just show how impoverished our public discourse has become. In fact, there are millions of American Christians who would not be able to tell the difference between a Ford F150 and an F350, and it doesn't take a Christian to look askance at the dung-based shock tactics that today pass for "art."

But nuance isn't the only thing lost when the broad brush of generalization is applied to the stretched canvas of public discourse, resulting in the derivative oil painting of ignorance. An entire group of Christians is lost in the mix. Sure, Grown-Up Hippie Christians may not have the kind of trappings that make other Christians so mediagenic: no wrestling leagues, no inspirational football

---

[2] This term is often misunderstood and regarded as pejorative because of some negative connotations of the word "low." In fact, it's a reference to the fact that many Protestant churches were built very close to the ground because of that denomination's historic fear of heights. Even today, the ceilings of many Baptist churches remain unpainted, because no one wants to get up on a ladder.

[3] This is a nonsense word invented by mischievous Greeks.

movies, no lawyer-fueled campaigns of bile at Christmas. But they're just as much a part of the landscape as their more prominent cousins, and their faith bears just as many imprints of popular culture, just not the wrestling, auto-racing, rock-for-Jesus kind.

GOD'S HIPPIE DINOSAURS

Although it may seem hard to believe in today's era of high-profile evangelical personalities and blockbuster movies about Jesus, the GUHC was actually the dominant type of Christian as recently as forty years ago.

Up until the 1960s, most Americans were affiliated with what are known as the "mainline" churches, because they were all founded in or near Philadelphia. These were the historical denominations of traditional Protestantism: the Episcopalians, the Lutherans, the Congregationalists, the Presbyterians, some of the Methodists,[4] a couple of Baptists, the CIA, and the Churches of Christ.

Not to put too fine a point on it, but these were the churches people thought of when they thought of the word "boring." They were the churches in the grey flannel suits; the buttoned-down, straitlaced churches with a crease in their trousers and a book full of hymns written by one of the Wesley brothers.[5] They embodied a peculiarly middle-class, American version of Christianity, one that revolved around the twin commandments of bringing a covered dish to potluck and not making a scene.

The mainline churches became dominant in America after a series of religious controversies in the early part of

---

[4] Not the shouting ones.
[5] John, Charles, and Wesley.

the twentieth century that pitted science-loving fanatics against people from the South. The most famous of these was the Scope Monkey Test, which centered around the question of which mouthwash would best improve apes' breath. For some reason, the trial involved former Democratic presidential nominee Adlai Stevenson, who argued with Spencer Tracy about whether you could leave someone the weather in your will.[6]

After this debacle, the more traditional (read: Southern) Protestants withdrew from public life for several decades. The field was left to the mainline churches, and their theological concept of God was probably something like your boss, except less likely to drink Scotch at lunch.

In the 1960s, though, everything changed, as it was generally wont to do in the Sixties. Along with the revolutions in civil rights, education, gender relations, mass media, popular culture, and ugly flatware came a revolution in religion. The stodgy, boring mainline churches — the very exemplars of all that was sedate, square, and unhip — suddenly went from gray flannel to tie-dye and love beads, forever changing the characters of their traditional denominations.

Unfortunately for them, they also lost about half their members and virtually disappeared from the public square. But — contrary to received wisdom — they did not vanish altogether in an ill-fated wagon train to the Pacific Northwest. Instead, like their traditionalist (read: Southern) cousins decades before, they simply retreated from the harsh glare of the spotlight to reorganize, refocus, and eventually re-emerge, stronger and more vital than ever.

---

[6] As summed up in the famous play about the case, *You Can't Inherit The Wind, Charlie Brown.*

So who are these Grown-Up Hippie Christians, and what do they believe? The answers may shock and enlighten anyone who believes that Christianity is nothing more than sweating televangelists and homeschooled lawyers threatening to sue over the absence of Christmas carols in a school play.

First, although the GUHCs have their largest base in the mainline churches, not all GUHCs are members of those denominations. In today's increasingly "post-denominational" world, a GUHC can be a Catholic, a Unitarian, an especially confused Jew, or even one of the oatmeal-loving paragons of pacifism known as Quakers.[7] They can even have no denominational affiliation at all, believing that God is best accessed outside the traditional confines of churches, religious organizations, and other places that make you get up early on Sunday morning.

The GUHCs, then, are a diverse group, encompassing everyone from East Coast English degree recipients to West Coast literature degree recipients, and the odd philosophy major in between. They are people who, contrary to the stereotype about middle-class products of liberal arts universities living within walking distance of at least three Starbucks outlets, are actively committed to a relationship with God but who find the traditional spiritual options unsatisfying. They are also passionately committed to the affairs of the world, finding the greatest resonance in Jesus' call to visit the prisoner, nurse the sick, and vote for the city council candidate opposed to big-box stores.

Even a trained Internet Theologian, though, has to

---

[7] Or, as they are called in their native Pennsylvania, "Shakers."

be cautious about making generalizations. GUHCs prize individuality above all else and insist that their unique paths to God are journeys that can only be made alone. But we can, with some due caution, make a few observations about the way GUHCs interpret the Christian tradition that stand in sharp contrast to the beliefs and practices of their more orthodox ("Southern") coreligionists.

1 THIS IS A JUDGMENT-FREE ZONE. It's very important for the GUHC to avoid laying a guilt trip on anyone, except those who happen to drive sports utility vehicles. The purpose of Christianity, after all, is not to cast blame or make people stop doing things that may be harmful to themselves; it's to celebrate that which makes you distinctively *you*. If that means sleeping in on Sundays and communing with God by doing yoga out back in the Meditation Garden, it's hard to imagine Jesus having a problem with that. And if that means participating in the World's Largest Gang-Bang, Part 2, then, hey: follow your bliss, and it will lead you to Truth. If, however, that means driving a Hummer, you're out of luck, sinner.

2 GOD DOESN'T LIVE IN CHURCHES. He lives outside, in the open air with the birds and the animals and the homeless; he lives in our kitchens, when we have a raucous dinner party to celebrate the release of a new Michael Moore movie at the art house cinema; he lives in our bedrooms, our magnet schools, and in the kitchens of our favorite fusion cuisine restaurants. Getting out of church can often mean getting in touch with God; it can also mean not having to spend Sunday morning with a bunch of people you don't even know after getting up at a truly ungodly hour. And

don't get me started on how crowded the pews get at Christmas.

3 THE BIBLE IS A MAP; IT'S NOT THE TERRITORY. Sure, there are some great things in the Bible: the Sermon on the Mount, Mary Magdalene getting elected the first pope, and the part where Jesus talks about the need to support community radio. But there are also some pretty negative vibes in that book: war, slavery, genocide, child abuse in the form of near-sacrifices, animal abuse in the form of actual sacrifices. It's pretty hard to square a lot of that stuff with the *real* message of Jesus.[8] Besides, most of that was written thousands of years ago; we can't possibly expect it to serve as a reliable guide for contemporary Christians. For that, you'll have to make your own "Bible," containing works that *you* think are important and spiritually insightful, preferably including something by Malcolm Gladwell.

4 COME AS YOU ARE; GOD'S JUST GLAD YOU MADE IT. Somewhere in the Bible, Jesus says, "I am the way, the truth, and the life. No one comes to the Father but through me." Obviously, either a later chronicler tampered with those words, or Jesus was speaking on Opposite Day, because he couldn't have possibly meant something so exclusionary. Jesus' whole message was about radical inclusion: women, men, lepers, Samaritans—everybody was invited to his heavenly party. All paths to God are worthy, since all contain the essential truth of God's message. Jesus, Buddha,

---

[8] "The love you take is equal to the love you make," as it says in the Gospel of John.

Mohammed, L. Ron Hubbard—they all had pretty much the same thing to say: "Be cool to each other." It's ridiculous to imagine that God cares whether someone's Catholic, Protestant, or Zoroastrian. If Jesus were here today, he'd say, "All my children are good in my sight. Here, have some fair trade coffee. It's from Botswana."

5   THE CHALLENGE OF JESUS: WALK IT LIKE YOU TALK IT. When Jesus chastised the Pharisees, Sadducees, and Referees, it was because they were too caught up in arguing about minor doctrinal points, like whether there's an afterlife, to do the *real* work of religion: namely, building vegetarian soup kitchens, donating books to the local penitentiary, and writing letters to the state legislature demanding an immediate change in same-sex marriage laws. Jesus didn't want people sitting around worshiping him; he wanted them to get out there and give that jabbering homeless guy a bowl full of vegetarian chili. Focus on service, and don't sweat the small stuff, like the afterlife.

As we can see from this list, there are several crucial ways in which the GUHC stands apart from Christians who are concerned with things like "tradition" and "orthodoxy" and "the Bible." And because those other Christians have captured the imagination of the American public, the GUHC has been relegated to the shadows.

This twist of popularity is ironic, because the GUHCs' ideas about God, religion, and the mellow, laidback, first-century hippie known as Jesus Christ are arguably far more influential in popular culture at large than the ideas of the more tradition-minded Christians.

Take, for example, the fact that surveys routinely

show huge percentages of Americans who believe in
eternal damnation also expressing the utmost confidence
that they themselves will not personally suffer such an
unpleasant fate.[9] This serene confidence is foreign to the
more traditional branches of Christianity. Martin Luther,
the Elvis Presley of Protestantism, was positively fixated
on questions about the fate of his soul. Arguably, if he had
any of the confidence most Americans display about their
destination in the afterlife, there never would have been a
Protestant Reformation—and, tragically, this book never
would have been written.

Luckily for us, then, Luther was morbidly fixated on
hell. But the GUHCs—like most Americans—are not. The
affinities, though, don't stop at the gate marked "Abandon
all hope, ye who enter here."

Like the GUHC, most Americans are uncomfortable
with exclusivity, whether in terms of country club member-
ships or soteriology.[10] That's why the notion—embraced
explicitly by GUHCs—that there are many paths to God
is so attractive to most Americans, to the point where
many of them attribute this concept to the actual doctrines
of world religions, which are, needless to say, a bit more
rigorous when it comes to such matters. Americans simply
don't want to believe that their neighbors—the Rasmussens, who feed the cats when Americans are on vacation
and always bake an apple pie at Thanksgiving—are going
to fry eternally in a boiling lake of fire because they omit

---

[9] I read this in *Time* magazine while on an airplane once. It's
possible I dreamed it, but it rings true, and in the world of high-
level scholarship, that's what counts the most.

[10] This is a ten-cent word professors and scholars like to
use to make themselves feel important. It means, "relating to
religious stuff."

the words "and the Son" when reciting the Nicene Creed at church on Sunday. The Rasmussens seem like such nice people, and if it's only a matter of three little words—why, it's positively crazy to believe something like that matters to God.

It isn't only in the arena of beliefs that the GUHCs have exerted their covert influence on American culture, however. A movement that began within the scholarly circles of the GUHCs has since exploded in popularity and become almost as familiar a part of the American religious landscape as those fish bumper stickers. This movement has gone on to challenge established orthodoxies as no other phenomenon has since the dawn of the guitar Mass in 1972.

I am referring, of course, to the Gnostics,[11] the Grown-Up Hippie Christians of the second century.

It is not too much to say that America is currently undergoing a Gnostic Mania, similar to Beatle Mania but more popular with community college professors. Everywhere you turn, you can see the trappings of this fascination—in bestselling books like the *Da Vinci Code*, and also in films extolling the virtues of such previously obscure works as the Gospel of Thomas; in travel package tours of sacred Gnostic sites, many of which are, happily, located in the South of France; in church book clubs suddenly discussing a heretofore-unknown canon called the Gnostic Gospels; and in the ubiquity of pseudoscholarly tomes promising to provide insight into the complex world of first-century Christianity, often with the aid of invented dialogue.

Truly, the Gnostics have come a long way from being

---

[11] Pronounced "Guh-NO-sticks."

Christianity's first wackjobs. For centuries unknown outside the ivory tower circles of scholars and church historians, the Gnostics have been thrust into the center of
popular religion. But is their reappearance—some seven-
teen hundred years after their beliefs were first chortled
out of existence by the orthodox—a genuine sign of historic consciousness, or just a desire to find ancient sources
for contemporary positions?

To answer this question, we have to first look at who
the Gnostics were and why they insisted on starting their
name with a silent "G."

THE GNOSTICS
FIRST-CENTURY APOSTLES OF MELLOW

The Gnostics were a band of loosely organized—even
unconnected—Christians who, starting in the late first
century (or possibly earlier, or possibly later—this is why
the so-called scholars are losing credibility; they can never
get their dates right), challenged the emerging consensus
about Jesus' being extolled by the party organized around
Paul, James, Peter, and other early Christians who died
in genuinely horrific ways.

At root was the Gnostic contention that the material
world was evil and that only the spiritual side of human
beings was capable of attaining salvation. To this end, the
Gnostics argued that Jesus himself had not been a human
being but had been, rather, a sort of ghost. They argued
that Jesus wasn't really crucified, that someone else[12] was
executed in his stead. The point was that the flesh was

---

[12] An unfortunate winner of a Jesus Look-a-like Contest,
perhaps?

evil, so Jesus could not have been flesh.

They acknowledged that this view would be a minority taste. It was only available to those who had attained *gnosis*, a Greek word meaning "know-it-all," and therefore only those people could be saved. But in order to reach heaven, the soul would have to travel through a number of intermediate worlds, each guarded by fierce demigods known as "archons." These archons would only allow the soul passage if it retained knowledge of secret passwords.[13] The Gnostics consequently spent a great deal of time memorizing these, time which could arguably have been spent more profitably in, say, operating a successful chain of dry-cleaners.

Frankly, it's not hard to see why this school of thought didn't exactly catch on. Before long, the Gnostics and their secret passwords had fallen by the wayside, and the so-called orthodox Christians were faced with successive waves of new heretics, like the Montanists, the Arians, the Mugwumps, the Vegans, and the 1974 Philadelphia Flyers.

And there Gnosticism would have remained, an unintentionally hilarious early heresy known only to pale, out-of-shape scholar types shotgunning Red Bull in their wretched garrets while writing monographs to be read by no one. However, a series of fortuitous discoveries of old manuscripts left in the dirt in Egypt led to a reawakening in the twentieth century of interest in things Gnostic. Those documents—the so-called "Gnostic Gnospels"— have in turn fueled a popular belief that the Christianity that emerged in the fourth century was only one of several "lost Christianities" and that we'd all be better off if one of

---

[13] No fooling!

those had persevered instead. Although, probably not if the Donatists had won.[14]

But the Gnostics so revered by the GUHCs—and later, by anyone with a long enough airport layover to plow through the bulk of the *Da Vinci Code*—are quite different from the world-hating password geeks presented by mainstream scholarship.

Let me paint a picture for you: the GUHCs believe the Gnostics were practically children of the Age of Aquarius in the range of their social convictions and ideas about the organization of church and faith. They were protofeminists, appointing women to important leadership roles; egalitarian, arguing against the Roman institution of slavery; vegetarian, abstaining from any food that involved another being's suffering; tolerant, believing that there are many ways to reach enlightenment; and opposed to organized religion, which they felt polluted the truth of Jesus' message. Rather than be concerned with distant deities, they revered what Jesus the human being taught about the ways in which other human beings should be treated. And they collected all these beliefs in a series of remarkable documents that were suppressed by the institutional church for being too incendiary.

The only drawback to this picture is that it bears almost no relation to reality whatsoever. According to the killjoy mainstream scholars and their lame-o insistence on "documentary evidence," the Gnostics really were kind of an unpleasant bunch. Far from being interested in the stewardship of the planet, they regarded the material world as the creation of an insensate, sadist demiurge; whether they can be considered proto-feminists is over-

---

[14] They tended to be pretty grumpy dudes.

shadowed somewhat by their abhorrence of procreation. And as for the Gnostic Gnospels, when the influential Gnostic teacher Marcion[15] proposed a canon of Scripture, thereby kickstarting the orthodox effort to do the same, his proposal consisted of the Gospel of Luke and Paul's letters. Nary a Gospel of Harold among them.

This, though, has not stopped the construction of a narrative which has the original Christian teachings being passed down through the Gnostics to the Cathars, who were oppressed by the Catholic Church for supporting bottle deposit programs, and through them to Leonardo Da Vinci, who hid them in his paintings of men that look like ladies. Today, this narrative of suppression and secret survival is taken for granted by many people who don't otherwise know that much about Christianity. It's particularly useful for those seeking a precedent in historical tradition for ideas which are otherwise redolent of Beatle boots and be-ins.

The popularity of Gnosticism—which studies show far outstrips the popularity of any other Christian heresy, even Dynamic Modalism—is a pyrrhic victory for the GUHCs, though. Couched as it usually is in the language of historical scholarship (however inept), Gnostic Mania generally doesn't need to acknowledge its original popularizers in the seminaries of mainline churches.

That brings us to perhaps the central conundrum of the GUHCs' relationships with popular culture: the culture at large takes from the GUHCs, but gives almost nothing to them in return.

We've traced the extent of the debt which popular religion in America owes to the GUHCs; everything from

---

[15] Or, as he was known to his fellow Gnostics, Gmarcion.

Nonjudgmental Jesus the Social Worker to the idea of Christians, Muslims, and Parsees partying like it's 1999 in an eternal, Woodstock-like heaven can be said to come directly or indirectly from the GUHCs. And the Gnostics—who have inspired bestsellers as well as a curiously wooden Tom Hanks performance—have crashed into the center of popular culture thanks to the GUHCs' efforts to rescue them from the oblivion of historical accuracy. But do the GUHCs get any credit for its selfless toil on behalf of popular Christianity? Let's look at the facts.

Their GUHC numbers are shrinking each year. What's more, those GUHCs who remain tend to be old enough to remember who Harold Stassen was without having to look him up on Wikipedia.[16] And their media profile is lower than that of the average third-runner-up on "American Idol."

It would be one thing if they were losing out in media exposure to the Catholics alone. After all, the Catholics have the pope, a built-in celebrity who, like superstars Cher and Prince, generally has to use only one name. But when most Americans are asked to describe what they think of when they hear the word "Christian," studies[17] show they generally think of Evangelical Protestants, Catholics, or the sensational performance of actor Christian Slater as pirate radio DJ Mark Hunter in 1990's *Pump Up the Volume* before they think of GUHCs.

Grown-Up Hippie Christians have reacted to this state of affairs by attempting to use popular culture to explain themselves to the world at large and to attract new people to the faith. For some reason, though, they're much

---

[16] He cured polio.
[17] Source: studies.

better at influencing popular culture than being influenced by it. Whereas their ideas tend to translate very well to pop culture, the forms of pop culture seem awkward when crudely bolted onto the framework of the GUHC faith. It's roughly the same experience as having your cool high school English teacher read song lyrics as examples of poetry; in theory, it should work fine, but in practice you just feel embarrassed.

Although it may seem counterintuitive to say this about a milieu that produces Christian wrestling leagues, the independent research of the Internet Theologian has confirmed an irrefutable truth: the Evangelical Protestants generally commandeer pop culture much better than the GUHC.

It was one thing in the 1960s, when the cutting edge of pop apologetics was peopled by theological rebels young enough to make those shaggy haircuts and peace necklaces work. But there's nothing quite as mortifying as having your grandmother punctuate a Sunday sermon by strumming an electric guitar and crooning that Jesus wants you to get high with a little help from your friends.

When the wiseacres of the mainstream culture industry want to lampoon Christianity, they generally turn to the fringe of Evangelical Protestantism — staging reenactments of Hallowen "Hell House" plays, for example, or filming documentaries at Pentecostal summer camps. But for true cringe value, it's hard to beat a Hip-Hop Mass presided over by a fifty-six-year-old priest who delivers the entire sermon in what she clearly believes is the argot of African-American teenagers. It's the kind of spectacle that would make even Gmarcion Gvomit.

The real shame of it is, of course, GUHCs don't need to rely on such tactics. They've already proven their ability to influence popular religious discourse—all they need to do in order to turn their fortunes around is to go the extra mile and start claiming credit for such influence. This may not be a popular approach in a theological camp given to looking askance at marketing language, but the GUHCs should think in terms of branding.

Instead of issuing books on the Gnostic Gnospels and watching others reap the rewards, they shouldn't be afraid to run commercials proudly proclaiming ownership: "The Gospel of Thomas: Brought to You by the Christians That Host the Community Art Show Every Spring," the tagline could run. Or they could pass out little tracts that say things like, "Got a nagging feeling your Hindu neighbor is going to heaven? Well—*you're welcome.*"

The GUHCs have a winning product; the problem is that, for too long, they've sat back and watched other people reap the rewards of their hard work. When that comes to an end, you'll start to see their churches filling up again, and before long, when people hear the word "Christian," they won't just think of a Southern Baptist preacher fanning himself with a Bible at the Republican National Convention; they'll also think of their hippie English teacher with a picture of Charles Darwin on his desk.

At any rate, the GUHCs have to do something. They present us with the fascinating spectacle of a Christian group that has influenced culture rather than merely being influenced by it but that suffers from an inability to capitalize on that influence. Or, as St. Augustine famously sang, "You can't always get what you want."

Applying the Hypostatic Union to a Winning Zone Defense

The image of the Internet Theologian is surely awe-inspiring when it comes to his mental gymnastics, but he is considerably less so when actually engaging in physical activity. Many people imagine him[1] seated at a desk day and night, illuminated by the blue glow of his flat-panel monitor, going without sleep, exercise, or unsalted snacks solely to bring greater understanding to the benighted masses. This is pretty accurate.

But the jousting in the comboxes and chatrooms is, alas, purely metaphorical: no great physical specimen, the Internet Theologian frequently gets winded by the simple act of climbing stairs. The idea of lifting anything heavier than a cable modem fills him with dread. He is greatly relieved by the notion expressed in the Bible that the race is not to the swift, because frankly there are types of plants that can move faster than him. All told, you might be quick to conclude that the Internet Theologian is not a natural candidate for expertise in the fields of sport and athletics.

---

[1] Me.

But, just as you've been so many times in the past, you're wrong about that, too.

The Internet Theologian is not only a passionate sports fan, he brings to that realm all the autodidact's skill he learned in the harsh school of online theology. Because, in a world where there are millions of sports Web sites and where fantasy football leagues outstrip the number of actual emergency medical facilities, the Internet Theologian is utterly in his element.

Sports, after all, shares much in common with other Internet-friendly pursuits, like theology, music snobbery, and *Lord of the Rings* DVD trivia: a consuming aptitude for facts, figures, and entirely inconsequential minutiae.

There is, after all, little difference between the walking theology database and the walking sports database: the former must evaluate the complex arguments made by Protestants and Catholics about free will, while the latter judges equally challenging arguments about whether Ron Santo should be in the Hall of Fame.

But sports and Christianity are not merely two fields which require the same skills of Internet citizen-scholars. Although many people overlook them, the connections between the two are startling and pervasive, and luckily for me, they lend themselves extraordinarily well to a book like this.

CHRISTIANITY AND SPORTS
Not Just for Touchdown Jesus Anymore

Christianity and sports have been natural allies since Roman times, when Christians were frequent competitors in the gladiatorial games that so enthralled the ancient world.

Granted, extant box scores from the period have shown us that the Christians were pretty lousy athletes on average, repeatedly getting trounced by such mediocre Roman franchises as the Lions, the Gladiators with Weapons, and the Bags Filled with Snakes. But these early, mauled Christian athletes understood a crucial lesson about such games that escaped their contemporaries, particularly the animals: it doesn't matter whether you win or lose, what matters is how you play the game. Or, in this case, how you "play" while being sewn into a bag full of snakes and then set aflame for the delectation of mincing, sybaritic spectators wearing grapes in their hair.

Because of recent changes to U.S. law, athletic contests rarely result in death anymore.[2] But the excitement of athletic competition is as much a part of our society as it was in the Romans' day, and we have the added advantage of not being brain-damaged from drinking out of lead cups.

Yes, America is truly a sporting nation: from tender toddlers swinging away at T-ball games to the crustiest members of the PGA Senior Tour, it seems we just want to keep on playing sports until we drop dead. And not just playing, either; we are enthusiastic watchers of sports —all sports, even those which have been scientifically proven to be life-shorteningly dull spectator events, like golf. We are so sports-crazy we will even stop what we're doing every couple of years to watch people swim and ice-skate and throw something called a "discus"[3] and pretend it's sports.

---

[2] Another nanny-state intervention, courtesy of President Jimmy Carter.

[3] As a fun exercise, try to think of any time besides the Summer Olympics during which it is appropriate to use the word "discus."

Nor are we content to leave sports on the playing field, where they belong. As much as we like playing and watching sports, we are perhaps even fonder of applying lessons from sports to our daily lives. Not lessons like "When a basketball coach tells his point guard to stay out of the paint the next time the opposing team gets the ball, it probably means there's a hard foul coming," because lessons like that have limited daily application at best.

Instead, we want our conduct on the playing field, in the stands, or in front of the local judge after celebrating a World Series victory with arson to guide our conduct in other areas of life. We've all heard the expression "be a good sport," whether it's referring to taking a brutal drubbing at the hands of the two-hundred-million-dollar New York Yankees payroll or losing your fiancé to a guy named Chip who does something called "systems analysis." This is because being a good sport is universally recognized as better than being a poor sport, particularly if that designation involves setting Chip's car on fire.

In addition to applying lessons from the playing field to our lives, we look to athletes to provide us with role models. Who among us doesn't admire the stoic courage of Lou Gehrig or Brian Piccolo in the face of death? Or Dock Ellis's ability to pitch a no-hitter against the Padres while tripping on acid? In an era when politicians are oily crooks, movie stars are sexless cult freaks, and artists are relegated to the oblivion they have always deserved, athletes are our last real heroes.

These heroes, the lessons they teach us, and the rap CDs they foolishly record in the off-season exist in an arena of American life that is purely secular, according to conventional wisdom. But, just as in medieval times, when Columbus proved the earth revolved around the sun and was banished to Haiti because of it,[4] the Internet Theologian here invokes Rule Number One: conventional wisdom is for chumps.

In fact, sports offer an exciting and expanding terrain for the interplay of Christianity and popular culture, a terrain in which Jesus is credited with devising winning plays and in which the Christian athlete movingly relates a personal tale of struggle from sin and failure to gospel truth and victory (or hires a ghostwriter to do so).

But before we can examine the connections between sports and Christianity with the rigor characteristic of the Internet Theologian, we must first deal with some objections. And in characteristic Internet fashion, we will do so by lazily aiming our ad hominem attacks at strawmen.

Although sports fans are, on the whole, pious and devout in their religious faith,[5] many of them are nonetheless uncomfortable with the injection into sports discourse of any philosophical outlook more complicated than that of Yogi Berra. This breed of sports fan will devote far more thought and attention to athletic competition than to, say, their personal finances, but they will scream in horror at any attempt to bring nonsports concepts to bear on their beloved pastime.

If, for example, black athletes or fans try to discuss the damaging legacy of racism and legal segregation in contemporary sports, the Ignorant Sports Fan will immediately shout that race has nothing to do with sports because everyone had to retire Jackie Robinson's number. If feminists suggest that there are troubling attitudes toward women in a fan demographic that can be success-

---

[4] More or less.
[5] Source: the Society of Pious, Devout Christian Sports Fans.

fully pandered to by the suggestion that a particular light beer will enable them to have sex with twin sisters simultaneously, the Ignorant Sports Fan will clamp his hands to his ears and hum the Ohio State fight song rather than listen. And if a Christian athlete begins discussing how Jesus enabled him to finally develop a crossover dribble that is impossible to guard against, the Ignorant Sports Fan will huffily retire to the concession stand for a nine dollar hot dog and an outsized foam finger that proclaims the Broncos are Number One.

The bulletin boards, comment boxes, and letters sections of all the major sports Web sites — and, Lord knows, the shadier, unregulated precincts of fan-run sites — are full of missives from the Ignorant Sports Fan, arguing that all sport can be reduced to simple elements like winning, losing, and going to the bathroom during the fifth inning (the "beer inning"). Well, Ignorant Sports Fan, meet your nemesis: the Internet Theologian can be terrifying when his ire is raised.

The Ignorant Sports Fan will generally insist that sport is a Simple Thing and that to complicate it with Unsimple Things such as race, gender, or faith is to sully the sport in such a way as to make it as contentious and unpleasant as politics or trying to find parking at the mall in December. For the Ignorant Sports Fan, the only acceptable sports profundity is found in the Zen koans of coaches like Vince Lombardi, who only thought about football his entire life, who probably talked about football at his daughter's wedding, and who famously summed up his entire weltanschaung by saying, "Winning isn't everything. Wait, yes it is."[6]

---

[6] Some may object that this is not a verbatim rendering of what Lombardi said, to which the Internet Theologian replies: write your own book.

At the risk of sounding overcritical, not only is the Ignorant Sports Fan's argument completely asinine, but he looks like a child wearing those shorts and a baseball cap turned the wrong way around. For God's sake, it's supposed to keep the sun out of your eyes, you man-boy.

Sport—similar to other complicated human activities, like warfare and shopping at Ikea—is in fact a microcosm of the wider society which gives it birth. Sports are a reflection of us as a whole, good, bad, or as terrible as the NFC North. And we are a society that at times seems deeply Christian in some respects, while at other times we resemble nothing so much as one of those empires in late antiquity that sacrificed virgins to the god of unpleasant footwear. A mess of contradictions, in other words.

With this in mind, it's only fitting that theology in sports resembles theology in society as a whole: confusing, contradictory, and an at-times incomprehensible hash of good intentions and terrible follow-through.

It is to that mishmash of mumbled good intentions and ceaseless passion for attributing success on the field to divine intervention that the Internet Theologian now turns.

THE CHRISTIAN ATHLETE
BRUSHING BACK BATTERS FOR JESUS

Long ago, Christians were suspicious of sports. Perhaps it was because of lingering institutional memories of persecution by the great Roman athletes of the second century. Perhaps it was because, early on, sports were dominated by foreign-seeming Catholics, like Babe Ruth. Or perhaps it was because most athletes were drunken, lecherous louts, like Babe Ruth.

Whatever the reason, the sporting world was seen as

inhospitable territory for faithful Christians, who were urged to express their passion for physical fitness and competition in other ways, such as missionary work and voting for William Jennings Bryant. This wariness persisted right up until professional athletes started making more money than the U.S. president, at which point many Christians began to heed Paul's advice: "Thou shalt not shun a good racket, particularly if it means avoiding the prospect of actual labor."[7]

But Christians refused to conform to the wicked ways of sports—rather, they would themselves act as a "salt ministry," leavening the bread of rough and tumble athletics with the yeast of discipleship.

Thus was the Christian Athlete born.

However, making sports safe for Christians was not as easy a task as ignoring hockey until the Stanley Cup finals. At first, in fact, the Christian Athlete had a difficult time in the hard and unforgiving realm of sports. Something about the athletic life led naturally to excessive drinking, casual sexual relationships, and sliding hard feet first into second, so as to "spike" unwary opponents. The temptations were great for a Christian Athlete, and many people started out in the Major Leagues of Sanctification only to be called back to the Triple A Club of Sin to work on their Bat Speed of Forebearance.

As newspaper editor and Methodist James Carty lamented to *Time* magazine in 1957 (the August 19 issue), "Nothing counts but victories, no matter how achieved. I

---

[7] Mainstream scholars will probably argue that Paul said no such thing. If you've read this far, you probably know how much stock the Internet Theologian puts in the opinions of mainstream scholars. My offer stands, gentlemen: I'm ready to arm wrestle you at any time, in any venue you choose.

have searched long, diligently—and in vain—to find more than one individual who is outstanding both as an athlete and layman." (Ironically, the one individual he had found who was outstanding on both counts was Mike Tyson.)

Before long, though, a number of alliances formed at amateur and professional levels, designed to strengthen the resolve of the Christian Athlete by creating a band of dedicated believers who were convinced that the gospel and the sports pages need not be mutually exclusive. The Fellowship of Christian Athletes, Christian Sports International, and John Wooden's UCLA Bruins all sprang into existence, offering succor and aid to athletes battered by the temptations of the sporting life.

And it wasn't long before the Christian Athlete went from being as rare as a consistent knuckleball pitcher to being as familiar a presence on the sports landscape as a college basketball coach in a cheap suit.

But just what is a Christian Athlete?

At the most basic level, he or she is an athlete who "gives the glory to God," in the language of innumerable pieces of evangelistic literature. There are many, many tracts, books, DVDs, and seminars by or about Christian Athletes—including All Stars, Pro-Bowlers, and whatever the hockey equivalent is[8]—that stress this aspect of sports ministry.

---

[8] Full disclosure: I haven't considered hockey a sport since the Hartford Whalers left town for a state where it is too warm to play hockey without artificial refrigeration. The existence of teams in Arizona, Florida, and Southern California is not helping hockey's cause with me. I might as well also take this opportunity to list other pursuits that I don't consider sports: golf, tennis, auto racing, ice-skating, running, skiing, boxing, skateboarding, riding bicycles in an unsafe manner, roller derby, and ballroom dancing. Candlepin bowling is still okay, though.

What this means, in practice, is that Christian Athletes will often credit God with bringing their team a hard-fought victory, particularly in championship contests. Christian baseball players will, after hitting a clutch home run, often point skyward, as if to direct the crowd's attention to the *real* slugger, while Christian football players will, in the glow of a post-Super Bowl victory interview, often thank God even before thanking the left tackle.

This, though, raises a thorny theological question: If God wants Team A to win, does that mean he wants Team B to lose? In other words, why don't Christian Athletes blame God for a loss? Surely God is just as responsible for causing the inexplicable fumble in the last seconds of the game as he is for the fumble's miraculous, game-winning recovery. This is the prickly and difficult territory of theodicy, the dilemma of evil in a monotheist religion, which was famously summed up in the title of a bestselling book: *Why Do Good Things Happen to Yankees Fans?*

If pressed, the Christian Athlete will point out that he doesn't think God actually cares about the outcome of a sporting event, not even when UConn plays Syracuse at the Carrier Dome. The reason for invoking God after a victory is to draw attention to the Lord's role in shaping the athlete into the kind of competitor who is capable of making the kinds of plays that win big games—and making them in a manner consistent with gospel teachings on meekness and humility.

This brings us to the second major peculiarity of the Christian Athlete—the idea that Christianity should inform the type of play, to the point where a Christian Athlete's style is markedly different from his colleagues' heathenish rumbling.

The handful of Web sites I browsed on the topic were

vehement in stressing the importance of applying Christian virtues to athletic competition. Or they seemed to be, anyway: there was a hilarious rerun of *Golden Girls* on TV that distracted me from my "e-search."

One Web site that celebrated the exploits of a Christian running back in the NFL, describing his play as "unshowy—he doesn't hog the limelight with a lot of flashy maneuvers."

Thus, the ministry of a Christian Athlete doesn't just consist of giving God props at post-victory press conferences; the Christian Athlete also exhibits a certain style of play on the field. Such behavior is what's known as "the evangelism of the good example." A Christian Athlete is one who doesn't cheat, commit fouls, whine to the ref, hog the ball, engage in copious end zone dancing, taunt opponents, spit on fans, or skip practice in order to sulk because the coach won't let him wear ten pounds of platinum jewelry on the field.

A Christian Athlete, in other words, is incredibly dull.

Who wants to go and watch a basketball game where no one cries to the referee, pretends to be more hurt than he or she is, or throws a forearm in that uppity point guard's face when the ref is distracted?

The Christian Athlete would do well to look at the most popular sports-related viral videos on the Web: not much "unshowy play," there, fellas, but a whole heck of a lot of entertaining brawls that spill into the crowd.

All this "unshowy play" stuff, if taken too far, can lead to severe practical consequences for the quality of the game. As we all know, Jesus, when giving the Apostles the Ten Amendments, included "Thou shalt not steal" among them. Does this mean that Rickey Henderson and

Alvin Robertson[9] are going to hell?

If worse comes to worst and the Christian Athlete is both a showy player and someone who habitually forgets to thank Jesus for making the pitcher throw one right over the plate when the count was 3-0, he still has one fallback strategy: the redemption narrative.

Redemption is one of the ideas central to Christianity, along with potlucks and not sleeping in on Sundays. Any redemption narrative will resonate with all but the most wishy-washy Christians, and a redemption narrative from a professional athlete is even more potent, because it gives those of us who are too fat to compete in any sport except candlepin bowling the ability to feel superior to a famous millionaire in peak physical condition.

I have digested the outlines of *several* such stories and as such can confidently chronicle the basic format of a Christian Athlete's redemption narrative:

> *There I was, sitting in my multimillion dollar, jewel-encrusted home on a cliff overlooking the ocean, five Super Bowl rings weighing down my fingers, several fashion models cleaning my pool—and I was preparing to end it all by sewing myself into a bag full of snakes.*
>
> *How did I, Jake Q. Handsome, star quarterback, get this low? Oh, sure, I had everything—the adulation of millions, fast cars, big house, unintentionally hilarious oil paintings of myself as some kind of country squire. I even had Shaquille O'Neal's number on speed dial.*
>
> *But inside, away from the fans and the TV lights and*

---

[9] Respectively, the record holders for most stolen bases in major league history (1,406) and the most career steals in the NBA (a phenomenal 2.71 per game). They failed to heed the words of the Decalogue and must learn the awful truth: the record book is not the same as the Book of Life.

the soup endorsements, I was dying. Every time I walked out on the field and racked up three hundred passing yards against the hapless Phoenix Cardinals, I said to myself, 'Three hundred yards—and I feel like I'm going nowhere.'

I was missing something, but I didn't know what. That's when I met Pastor Skip. We were both at an airport waiting for a flight, and he leaned over and gave me what looked like a small comic book.

"Here, friend," he said. "You look like you need this."

Of course, I had my bodyguard beat him to a pulp and throw him out of the airport. But later, that night, I read it. It was a Bible tract, and it told me that I was hurt—hurt with sin. And that God had put in the ultimate substitute to play for me—Jesus. I fell down on my knees right there and asked Jesus to enter my life.

Later, I paid for Pastor Skip's facial reconstruction surgery.

The redemption narrative can be a powerful tool, allowing Christian Athletes not only to offer personal testimony about the effect of God's love on their lives, but also to bypass questions about why their styles of play have earned them nicknames like "The Filthy Weasel."

Note, though, that the redemption narrative will not always have the powerful, transformative effect the Christian Athlete intends. It's really a device best suited to certain professional athletes, and by that, I mean professional athletes who are actually good at their sports. No one wants to read the gripping account of a competent but unspectacular second basemen's dark night of the soul.

This caveat is even more true of college sports and, also, "fake sports" like ice-skating, marathon running, and hockey. Christians in those sports are advised to keep their redemption to themselves: you'll never sell Book One, folks.

To be fair to the Christian Athlete, he has a limited platform from which to glorify God and witness to the majesty of the Resurrection. A Christian composer, for example, can write a requiem Mass that endures as long as people listen to music. A Christian author can pen a novel that dares to look at the grace and majesty of God in his dealings with humans. A Christian painter can improve on those paintings of Jesus that make him look like a hippie in soft focus. An Internet Theologian can correct some dolt's misspelling of "Theotokos" in a Livejournal posting.

But a Christian Athlete really has to think long and hard about how the perfectly executed suicide squeeze reflects on the unfathomable majesty of the Almighty. Or whether tapping one's chest with three fingers and looking skyward after throwing down a meaningless slam dunk with ninety seconds left in garbage time is an effective means of evangelization.

So, in sum, the Christian Athlete must rely on three primary avenues for spreading the gospel: post-game press conferences, ghostwritten redemption narratives, and not taking forty shots a game. This limitation is in direct contrast with the other great figure of religious athletics, the Christian Coach.

THE CHRISTIAN COACH
GOD'S FOUL-MOUTHED PSYCHO

At first blush, no one in amateur or professional athletics seems less qualified to act as an ambassador for Jesus than the coach. Indeed, our society as a whole has few less likely role models for such a post. Even arsonists have a certain air of solemnity that the coach lacks.

The sports coach is an unlikely candidate for such a role simply because all coaches have essentially two moods: sullen and shouting. Either they are brooding on the bench with their caps pulled low over their eyes or they are spitting with rage at the crimes against humanity committed by the referee who didn't notice a lane violation by the other team. These are not salubrious moods for Christians.

As Defensor Grammaticus recorded in *The Book of Sparkling Sayings*,[10] "Sullen, angry eyes betray the anger of the heart. In the soul that keeps the score of evils done to it, there dwell wolves." Had he been thinking of sports coaches, he might have added, "In the soul that keeps score of fouls committed by the other team but missed by the refs, there dwell psychotic badgers with incredibly foul breath."

The fact that most coaches are demented rage monkeys is not all that separates them from a traditional understanding of a Christian demeanor. Coaches are also the first people to compare what they do to warfare, and they regard athletics with a ferocious gravity not normally seen outside the sacks of major cities by Roman legionnaires. So how to reconcile these characters with Jesus, whose message was peace, peace, and more peace?[11]

Once again, through tireless efforts, the Internet Theologian has crafted a comprehensive and sagacious

---

[10] A work that, despite its promising title, consists mostly of motor vehicle maintenance tips.

[11] Except for the stuff about "I come not to bring peace, but a sword." Modern scholars agree the Pharisees missed a golden opportunity when they didn't brand Jesus a "flip-flopper" on key issues like this one.

answer to this challenging paradox, largely by typing the words "Christian coaches" into search engines.

The reason, my e-search has uncovered, that coaches are inclined to regard each game as a defense of Constantinople against the Ummayad hordes instead of a grown-up version of a child's game played by the semi-literate for the edification of the sedentary is that, unlike players, coaches understand with Vince Lombardi that "Winning isn't everything, in the same way that blood circulating through your body technically isn't 'everything.'"[12]

That's because if players are terrible, they will simply be traded to the New York Knicks, whereas coaches will lose their jobs and possibly have to go into career fields where men in their fifties are discouraged from wearing cleats and baseball caps. And nobody wants that, least of all the coaches.

But, despite these paradoxes, the world of coaching has opened itself up to Christian evangelizing so that today it's almost rare to come across the old breed of cheap suit-wearing, foul-mouthed coach ready to curse God and the heavens for last night's loss to Memphis.[13]

There are networks of Christian coaches that bring together men who would otherwise spend the off-season praying for each other's deaths; there are books about ways in which Christian ministry can be effectively integrated into a winning zone defense; there are seminars in which successful Christian coaches explain their philosophies on winning (run the ball) and how these relate to their faith (Jesus would run the ball).

What the coaches are doing is actually common

[12] I hope this satisfies the pedants who objected to my earlier rendering of the famous Lombardi maxim as "inaccurate."

[13] Memphis! The biggest jokes in the league!

throughout society. In plain terms, Jesus actually says very little about sports in the Bible.[14] But coaches who take Jesus' earthly ministry as a blueprint for winning the state championship are doing nothing that, say, politicians and political activists don't do just as frequently.

The act is literally one of re-creation, of making a "canon within a canon," although readers should not be concerned: these canons don't shoot anything. Instead of seeing Christianity as a religion of humility, meekness, and renunciation, Christian coaches are able to read different aspects of the tradition so that it becomes a message of diligence, discipline, and wind-sprints.

Search the literature of the Christian coaching movement and before long you'll encounter these words from 2 Timothy1:7: "For God did not give us a spirit of cowardice, but rather a spirit of power and of love and of self-discipline." This is pretty much the slam dunk quote of Christian sports.

And while other passages could be found in the New Testament to contradict this one, that's probably true of everything in the book. As a wise Christian scholar[15] once noted: "The reason for so many mistaken ideas about God consists solely in the inability to interpret Scripture in a spiritual sense. It has been taken in its literal sense only."

So in a context where the Bible and Christianity exist to be selectively interpreted, it's not ridiculous for someone to say the Bible offers important lessons about when it's a good idea to steal second. It may, however, be ridicu-

---

[14] Although the apocryphal Gospel of Thomas records him as disliking the designated hitter rule. This is just one of the internal clues that lead antiquarians to believe the book could not have been written before the middle of the second century.

[15] It was George "The Animal" Steele.

lous to think that God's okay with ordering one of your benchwarmers to commit a hard foul against the other team's three-point ace.

THE CHRISTIAN SPORTS FAN
BRINGING THE GOSPEL TO THE BLEACHER BUMS

One contradiction for the Christians sports fan is that the spectacle of contemporary sports may seem like more of a pagan entertainment than an opportunity for Christian evangelism. The sight of grown men and women slathering on colorful body paint, waving little banners, and cheering when the opposing team's quarterback gets hurt is not one recorded in patristic writing as signs of an illuminated soul. But if there's one thing we've learned about the patristic writers, it's that they could be real drips when it comes to harmless fun.

Into this seemingly inhospitable breach the Christian Athlete has leapt, followed by a legion of Christian coaches peddling memoirs, seminar engagements, and DVDs with titles like *Real Struggle, Real Victory*. Although not an unqualified success, integrating Christianity into American sports has brought much to be proud of and has arguably softened the image of professional athletes from the drunken inhabitants of regional jails to an elite of troubled, jewelry-encrusted superstars yearning for "something more."

But the transition is not complete. Sports is still a venue where Christianity's values and insights are not prized as highly as, say, the ability to throw a sharp, breaking bender of a curveball. If Christians are to truly remake sports, they will have to begin at the source of the discord, the ill-will, the rage—even, dare I say, the root of the sin.

I'm referring, of course, to the fans.

Although coaches have become twentieth-century-style "muscular Christians" and athletes have fully embraced the redemption narrative as the path to true success, the vast majority of sports fans remain a gang of bloodthirsty, baying lunatics, howling like the hordes of the Coliseum for more gore. If the play on the field and in the locker room is becoming Christianized, the stands are still rife with heathens.

No one who has ever been to a sporting event can deny this. Sitting in the stands when the home team is losing toward the end of a game is a little like being in the part of Hieronymous Bosch's *The Garden of Earthly Delights* that depicts hell. Except noisier.

The chaos in the stands take place at amateur events just as at professional games; in fact, the scenes are probably crazier at amateur games. There's nothing quite like parents enraged by a Little League coach's decision not to let their child pitch at a crucial moment for the team. In parts of the country, such roster disputes are occasionally resolved with tank battles.

We have come a long way from the days when athletes were considered the lowest of the low, plying their trade just to keep themselves in whiskey until the day came when they would be murdered by a jealous prostitute. Now, athletes are having pre-game prayer meetings with the other team, and coaches are sharing Bible quotes. Fans, however, are still smuggling in batteries in case they need to throw something that hurts.

The task of today's Christian Athlete, then, is to evangelize the fans, to awaken in America's vast sports faithful the kind of self-awareness that sports stars have taken for granted ever since it stopped being acceptable to fanta-size publicly about decapitating a quarterback with a legal tackle.[16] They need to take evangelism from the sidelines into the stands and share with fans the sober truths about faith and behavior, truths they've painstakingly learned in training camps, on championship teams, and as perform-ers of vanity rap albums.

And there are positive signs that fans may welcome such an effort, despite a natural reluctance to listen to any sports discussion deeper than "If we score more points, we will win." There was, for example, that weird guy in the rainbow wig who always came to games with the sign that said John 3:16; clearly, here's someone who under-stood the paradoxical nature of Christian sports fandom, in which one is moved to draw spectactors' attention to one of the most sublime verses in the Bible while simulta-neously pretending to have a rainbow-colored afro. There is probably no greater summation of the Christian sports paradox than this.

But of course we can't rely solely on lone crazies with wigs and signs. There must be newer, more creative forms of evangelism. Perhaps, during timeouts, when cheerlead-ers are using air guns to fire promotional T-shirts into the crowd, they could also fire tracts explaining why Jesus would frown on wishing that a referee would die in a grease fire.

Or maybe athletes could take time to meet with fans before the game, movingly describing their own faith jour-ney while also gently explaining the need to charge fifteen dollars per autograph (cash only, thanks).

---

[16] Dick Butkus, possibly the greatest linebacker of all time, actually shared such a fantasy. I am not aware of his writing a redemption narrative yet.

Or, perhaps—and this would be possibly the greatest single evangelistic measure of all—during a close and
crucial game, with the score tied, both teams could come
to the center of the field or the court[17] and put the ball
down.

They could then join hands and, addressing a hushed
crowd, movingly relate the gospel message of togetherness
and love for one another. Announcing that such a spirit of
unity and Christian friendship far surpasses the transitory
successes of the sporting world, they could then announce
that both teams have mutually decided the game will end
in a tie—a tie signifying the end of competitiveness and
the dawn of a new era in sports, where cutthroat attitudes
take a backseat to fraternal help and caring.

With the end of that announcement, they could lead
the crowd in a rousing rendition of "Bringing in the
Sheaves."

Such a moment would be an historic turning point for
sports, popular culture, and Christianity in America. It
would erase all memory of previous sports glories, showing them to be the distracting, ultimately meaningless
time-fillers they are. It would promote Christian fellowship in a radical way that most churches could only envy.

Actually, let's face it: It would end in a bloody riot and
lead to fines, suspensions, and the imposition of manda-
tory Zoroastrianism as the official faith of the NBA.[18]

We're a long way from the day when such a display

---

[17] But not the rink. Remember: hockey doesn't count any
more.
[18] When you think about it, Zoroastrianism is perfectly
suited to be the default faith of athletic competition—dualism,
and so forth. (Note: these are the kinds of sparkling insights
best attempted only by the trained Internet Theologian.)

of Christian sportsmanship would inspire anything in fans
other than murderous rage. After all, fans may not want
to talk about the underlying social, political, and religious dynamics of sports, but they've all done their best to
observe the famous statement of St. Paul, notably echoed
by Vince Lombardi:

"Winning isn't everything, but if you keep losing
season after season, don't be surprised when you end up
coaching the Knicks."

PAGE-TURNERS OF THE LAST DAYS

One of the great problems with the Old Testament is that it just trails off at the end. I mean, what happens, really? It's not even like one of those movies that has the words "The End?" at the closing credits, setting up the possibility of a sequel. It just sort of . . . stops.

No such problem exists for the New Testament. It brings everything together with a literally earthshaking conclusion that would be the envy of Hollywood's most imaginative screenwriter: Fire. Brimstone. Dragons. Heavenly hosts. Seas boiling. Skies falling. Locusts swarming. And best of all, the whole thing ends happily: the good guys win, and the bad guys end up intimately familiar with a molten lake of some kind.

This is all contained in the Apocalypse of St. John, also known as the Book of Revelation, or, among morons, the Book of Revelations.[1] Over the centuries, this work,

---

[1] Do an Internet search for "Book of Revelations" and prepare to lose faith in humanity. Along similar lines, I refuse to eat at any place that advertises "donut's."

attributed by Christians to St. John the Divine, has baffled, intrigued, and inspired countless heavy metal bands, as well as attracted comment from not a few religious types.

Here, for example, is prominent Protestant Reformer Martin "King" Luther on the book:

> "My spirit cannot fit itself into this book. There is one sufficient reason for me not to think highly of it—Christ is not taught or known in it."[2]

By contrast, here is what noted American theologian "Blind" Willie Johnson had to say on the same text:

> "Tell me, who's that writin'? John the Revelator. Tell me, who's that writin'? John the Revelator. John the Revelator wrote the book of the seven seals."

As we can see, reactions to the Apocalypse run the gamut[3] from baffled condemnation (Luther) to Mississippi Delta blues (Johnson). Perhaps no other part of the Bible has been as controversial down the ages; the Book of Revelation has inspired revolutions, tormented mystics, and freaked out hippies.

This is exactly the kind of dense, complicated, nuanced work best explained to the inquiring lay audience by the Internet Theologian.

Alas, I am not the only one in today's crowded marketplace of ideas offering to elucidate this text. Would that I were! The Internet Theologian would be filthy stinking rich.

---

[2] Luther, Works of Martin Luther, the Philadelphia Edition (Philadelphia, 1932), 6:489. Ha! There, you see? An actual footnote! Take that, critics who insist I am "habitually dishonest," "grossly ill-informed," and "seriously overweight!"

[3] Confession: I don't know what a "gamut" is, but I plan to keep using the word anyway.

Instead, I must do battle with a gamut[4] of authors who have taken up their pens and reinterpreted Revelation for a modern audience, seeking to make plain the work's references to everything from the European Union to the sexual potency of TV weathermen.

Inspired by the success of the *Left Behind* novels, apocalyptic fiction has pitched camp on our bestseller lists, roasting s'mores in the aisles of bookstores everywhere and lighting citronella candles in the hearts of readers.

In fact, experts estimate that sales of apocalyptic novels have now surpassed the one trillion mark[5] and continue to climb skyward. Millions of readers are taking the theological messages of these novels to heart, rather than going to "the source" and reading the Bible. This is largely because, let's face it, the apocalyptic stuff in the Bible is pretty much incomprehensible.

The muddled nature of Revelation has been important not only for today's bestselling apocalypticeers, but also for Christian scholars from time immemorial. Obviously, it's important for Christians to understand the Book of Revelation, since the bearded Greeks who assembled the biblical canon deemed it worthy of inclusion. But if you're working under the theory that the best way to interpret the Bible is to interpret it literally, Revelation presents some problems that, say, are not as noticeable in the Epistle of Jude.

As an idle exercise in textual criticism, let's take a look at a fairly straightforward passage from the Epistle of James:

---

[4] Is this the right way to use this word? It seems wrong somehow.

[5] Source: an especially vivid dream.

Do not speak evil against one another, brothers and sisters. (4:11)

Okay! Clear enough. We're not supposed to speak evil of our brothers and sisters, even when, say, our sister drops out of college and takes up with a two-bit "tattoo artist" and starts waitressing at Hooters. James isn't saying it's going to be easy, but at least you know what he means.

On the other hand, here's a characteristic passage from Revelation:

So when the dragon saw that he had been thrown down to the earth, he pursued the woman who had given birth to the male child. But the woman was given the two wings of the great eagle, so that she could fly from the serpent into the wilderness, to her place where she is nourished for a time, and times, and half a time. (12:13-14)

Got that? So, look out for that dragon, everybody. He's up to no good.

Throughout history, in fact, almost no one has interpreted Revelation literally. The most notable exception, of course, was the fourteenth-century Salesian monk known as Isaac the Credulous. His glosses on Revelation are considered valuable for historical interest, but they shed little light on the text itself, as they tend to consist entirely of marginal notations saying things like, "Whoa! A dragon! Scary."

Aside from Isaac, most theologians have chosen to interpret the book as symbolic of something: Joachim of Fiore, for example, thought it was a coded explanation of successive ages of world history, while Martin Luther believed it was a symbolic representation of how church history would unfold. Modified versions of Luther's theory are generally adopted by the bestselling authors of apocalypse fiction, although they tend to write more sex scenes than Luther.[6]

Generally, these works of popular fiction try to blend the literal with the more metaphorical approaches taken by interpreters like Luther and collectively ask: What would happen if the events described in Revelation were to happen in the contemporary world?

The resulting theme holds seemingly inexhaustible appeal, because readers can devour these fictions while imagining biblical prophecy as it applies to high-ranking politicians, glamorous starlets, and two-fisted TV meteorologists instead of boring Romans. In a way, the visceral appeal of these works leans heavily on Isaac's interpretation, but instead of "Whoa! A scary dragon!" they work more along the lines of "Whoa! A scary dragon — at the White House!"

Isaac the Credulous, though, was not much for subtext, whereas apocalyptic fiction thrives on the stuff. Yes, there are scary dragons, but, as these works make clear, the scary dragons will be unleashed by the machinations of charismatic European politicians, or possibly sinister corporate insiders, or in a pinch, overpaid professional athletes.[7] In this way, we can apply biblical lessons to our own lives without having to wonder why John the Divine would write, "a time, and times, and half a time," which seems awfully redundant. Was he being paid by the word out there on Patmos?

This modern, or "better," approach helps us work through the dense symbolism of the Book of Revelation

---

[6] And notably fewer sex scenes than Joachim, the old perv.

[7] See my forthcoming novel *Touchdown: Apocalypse!* for elaboration.

and see how God's plan for the end may play out in our time. It also gives the opportunity to experience vicariously the destruction of the Internal Revenue Service by some kind of horned beast, but that probably should be a secondary pleasure.

As an example of how these exciting works of popular fiction are changing the ways in which we interpret Scripture, let's take perhaps the most famous symbol in Revelation: the number 666. Here's what John says about it:

> This calls for wisdom: let anyone with understanding calculate the number of the beast, for it is the number of a person. Its number is six hundred sixty-six. (Rev 13:18)

John explains that everyone has to be branded on the right hand or the forehead with this mark, and if they don't have it, they are prohibited from buying and selling anything.

Here, then, is a particular challenge for literal interpreters of the Bible, particularly in a modern setting. Any government agency today suggesting a modest new program in which people are branded with the number 666 or banned from economic activity would be strikingly unpopular, even in Massachusetts.

This is no hurdle for popular writers of apocalyptic fiction, however, for they've devised a gamut[8] of possible explanations for what 666 could represent in our world. Some of the most popular are:

Bar codes: Those omnipresent charts of alternating thin and thick black lines are, in fact, the number of

---

[8] ????

the beast, for no one can "buy or sell" if their products are not affixed with bar codes. Unless they're buying, say, homemade jam from hippies at a roadside fruit stand in Vermont. This setup, though, raises the theologically untenable proposition that hippies are among the 144,000 saints mentioned in Revelation.

The Internet: Since the Hebrew letter "waw" roughly corresponds to "w," and since in gematria[9] "w" is the equivalent of six, then three w's together equal 666 — as in "www," the universal locator code for the World Wide Web! This is another reason people turn to the Internet Theologian: I sift through this garbage so you don't have to. The idea that the Internet could possibly be a tool of evil is clearly the product of someone who has never spent an afternoon using the mighty communications network as it was intended: to see grainy videos of famous people getting drunk and falling down.

Government: Since John says 666 is the number of a *person* rather than a demonic entity, we have to search the world of human beings for a likely candidate. And since in numerology six represents imperfection, it naturally stands to reason that John is referring to government. After all, is there anything less perfect than government? Just try getting that burnt-out streetlight in front of your house fixed. And gosh, don't those creeps down at the Highway Department act like they're oriental despots instead of a bunch of lazy, overpaid civil servants? Oh yeah; I can *definitely* see how 666 would refer to those guys.

---

[9] The ancient art of making coincidences seem weighted with meaning.

THE END OF THE WORLD
WILL YOUR FREQUENT FLYER MILES STILL BE GOOD?

The point is not that authors of apocalyptic fiction have the *correct* interpretation of this difficult passage, it's that by bringing the terminology up-to-date, they enable those of us who haven't wasted our lives on boring chores like learning Greek to have a say in what the Bible might mean.

Not that everybody's thrilled with the writers of popular apocalyptic fiction, of course. If you've been paying attention throughout this book, you probably won't be surprised by the news that egg-headed so-called scholars of religion have raised objections to what they consider sloppy theology, inaccurate interpretation, and laughably weak characterization and plotting. Not to mention those direct-to-DVD movies.

Since we're going to have to get around to this sooner or later, let's take up the carping complaints of Professor Boring Q. Dateless at the Institute of Snooze-ology and his ilk.

The most frequent complaint has to do with what is generally a starting point of end times fiction: the rapture.

No, this is not a reference to a song by Blondie, although that does figure heavily in some apocalyptic fiction.[10] The rapture doctrine hinges on a passage from Paul's First Letter to the Thessalonians: "Then we who are alive, who are left, will be caught up in the clouds together with them to meet the Lord in the air; and so we will be with the Lord forever" (4:17).

---

[10] See my forthcoming novel, *Hanging on the Apocalypse Telephone* for elaboration.

This is what's known as the "rapture," although Paul himself doesn't use that word. He uses the Greek term *harpazo*, but by common consent, rapture was chosen instead, because it sounds less like the name of a circus clown.

The rapture is what gives apocalyptic fiction its defining imagery of pilots suddenly disappearing from planes, drivers vanishing from behind the wheels of their cars, and parents leaving small children unattended in malls. Actually, it sounds kind of unpleasant, when you think about it like that. It sort of makes God out to be a kind of celestial kidnapper.

At any rate, the meaning of this passage from 1 Thessalonians is intensely disputed by Christians, who like to dispute everything intensely, more or less. My extensive researches (which stretched up to a full hour on the Internet one particularly boring day at work) have shown that within the camp of rapture believers are three major factions: pretribulationists, midtribulationists, and Shiites. Oh, wait, no: the third major faction is, of course, the post-tribulationists. The long-standing and bitter disputes between these factions center on (i) when the rapture will actually happen and (ii) which faction has the most unwieldy name. Briefly, their positions can be summarized thusly:

Pretribulationists believe that the rapture will occur prior to the Great Tribulation, which will itself be heralded by a Chicago Cubs vs. Boston Red Sox World Series and possibly by a telethon of some kind. According to this view, God's saints will be removed from the earth so as to miss all the scary parts in the Book of Revelation.

Midtribulationists believe that the rapture will occur right in the middle of things, when you've just sat down to dinner and are looking forward to unwinding after a tough day at work. And then, wouldn't you know it—boom!—you're ascending skyward without having a chance to tuck into your cheese tortellini. Talk about tribulation!

Post-tribulationists believe that not only will Christians have to endure all the most dragon-heavy parts of Revelation, but they won't get to enjoy the surprised looks on co-workers' faces as they are bodily assumed into heaven, just before things get really, really weird.

Part of the problem critics have with the doctrine of the rapture, as Professor Know-It-All of the Killjoy Institute for Fun-Ruining would undoubtedly point out, is that the rapture is not, in an extremely technical sense, actually *in* the Bible, if by "in" we mean "included in such a manner as to prevent the sorts of endless arguments that have characterized Christianity since the first Gnostic decided Jesus might have been a ghost."

Fortunately, you can disregard the eggheads, as you have the Internet Theologian at your disposal.

A number of Christian denominations maintain that the passage in Thessalonians refers not to any spectacular *harpazo* at all, but to the Parousia, or Second Coming of Christ.

The Bible, after all, promises a single return of Christ following his ascension into heaven: thus the Second Coming is what all Christians have traditionally looked forward to, unless it happens while they're in the midst of stealing cable or something.

The problem with pretribulationism is that it seems to propose a Third Coming of Christ, because Jesus shows up once for the rapture and then a second time at the end of the Tribulation. Pretribulationists usually get around this conundrum by insulting your mother.

And if that fails, they point out that there really isn't much biblical evidence for a mid- or post-tribulationist version of the rapture, to which the objecting Christian denominations say, "exactly," in kind of a smug way.

Shaky though its biblical foundations may be, pretribulationism, and the rapture in general, offer an irresistible "hook" for authors of apocalyptic fiction, giving writers a way to avoid all that nonsense about "wars and rumors of wars" that are supposed to come before the end of the world. In other words, it's a way to shave off a preface that would undoubtedly drag a bit and jump right into the action, usually featuring a heroic raft guide or TV news anchor.

And isn't that biblically sound? It makes sense to believe the end will start with little fanfare, right? How much advance notice do you expect?

Didn't Jesus say, "But about that day and hour no one knows, neither the angels of heaven, nor the Son, but only the Father"? And didn't he further say, "They shall be taken from their airplanes, their sport utility vehicles, and their playdates; amen, amen I say to you, they shall even be caught up while walking the dog, so as to provide a 'comic relief' scene where the poor hound yaps in confusion as it is lifted skyward along with its master"?[11]

For the novelist, though, the rapture presents a problem that is not only doctrinal: if God's saints are all

---

[11] No; he did not.

assumed bodily into heaven at the start of the Tribulation, what do you do for a main character? I mean, by definition, if all the saints are in heaven, who does that leave on earth? Wouldn't it be a motley collection of murderers, thieves, and trial lawyers? Who can root for those people? Demographic research, for instance, shows that most Americans are willing to shell out eighteen bucks for a novel that depicts nothing more than trial lawyers being pursued by locusts, for crying out loud. No one is going to read a book where the scum of the earth are also the heroes of the narrative.

This is not a problem for, say, the strict Calvinist end times novelist. After all, Calvin himself posited that decisions about salvation and damnation were more or less made completely at random by God so that, say, Don King could be lifted into heaven while Mr. Rogers is cast into an eternal lake of fire.[12] The market for strict Calvinist novels, though, is somewhere below the market for pro-Al Qaeda love poetry in terms of saleability, so prospective authors are cautioned to avoid it.

In fact, rather than run ourselves into a gamut[13] by considering all the theoretical problems and pitfalls with bestselling apocalyptic fiction, why don't we do a "hands-on" exercise and design our own? These apocalyptic novels are a license to print money right now, but you can never tell when the bottom's going to drop out, so as the Bible says, "strike while the racket is paying off."

---

[12] Seriously: Wasn't Calvin a nut?

[13] Note to editor: I'll look up the definition before this goes to press.

YOUR VERY OWN PATMOS
ONLY LUCRATIVE AND LIKELY TO HAVE
MULTIPLE SPINOFFS

One of the Internet Theologian's most guiding principles is "tell, don't show." I think that's also in various manuals on writing style, and possibly in the Articles of Confederation. At any rate, it's a most excellent rule of thumb, and so the Internet Theologian is going to *tell* you how to write your own apocalyptic fiction, rather than *showing* you his own outline for a novel. Because, let's be honest, you'll probably be so dazzled by my great ideas that you'll— even subconsciously—steal them.

The first step in crafting a successful apocalyptic novel is to forget immediately about taking anything straight from the Bible. Anyone seeking to hit a gold mine of inspiration in that dense and confusing tome is going to be disappointed. Sure, there are some nifty images in Revelation, but have you ever tried to read the whole book? I don't know if Luther's right about the spirit of Christ being absent from it, but clearly the spirit of coherence never got a toehold. Everything's a list of angels or trumpets or beasts, and by the time you get to the end, you'll be ready for a nap.

Besides (and this is crucial): *the public doesn't care what's in the Bible.* If I've learned one thing as an Internet Theologian, it's that if the public wanted to read the Bible, it would check into a Motel 6.

The Bible's the most readily available book in the world. That market is saturated. You have to give people what they can't get in the Bible itself: a coherent, linear narrative consisting of biblical ideas thrown together with storylines from action movies, plus a couple of good fight scenes. And a chaste kissing scene or two wouldn't hurt, depending on the target demographic.

Furthermore, don't worry about seeming "unlettered" or "inexperienced" or "completely unfamiliar with even the most basic tenets of the Book of Revelation." You'd be surprised at how much of Revelation you can pick up just by being a somewhat astute observer of popular culture. You've probably learned enough from those "Omen" movies to write a credible approximation of Bible-based foreboding.

Words and terms like "antichrist," "666," "the mark of the beast," and "Armageddon" are certainly not the exclusive purview of scholars these days. In fact, most of them have probably appeared in Def Leppard songs at some point.[14] My advice is to watch a bunch of horror movies about the Son of Satan or the Great Beast or something, take some notes, and maybe talk to your weird sister in that culty church that meets in a converted movie theater to discuss "signs of the last days."

Research thus completed, you now have to come up with a credible story unfolding along biblical lines. A good linear narrative starts off with a hero experiencing the shock of the rapture followed by the tyranny of the Tribulation, only to emerge in the victory of Christ's second, third, or fourth coming, depending on which market you're interested in saturating. He should also have a wisecracking African-American best friend.

Characters are crucial to the story since, God knows, doctrine isn't. The Internet Theologian's foolproof advice

---

[14] Certainly Armageddon has, in the song "Armaggedon It." Even though it's a pun, the song raises the prospect that Def Leppard is more biblically literate than most of its audience. Food for thought.

is to start with a good-natured, courageous male hero, preferably a TV newsperson of some kind. Scientific analysis has determined that TV newspeople make the best heroes for apocalyptic novels.[15] Give him a name that's forceful and catchy, but not derivative or ridiculous. Jason Danger is a good example of the kind of name you should use.

Nothing begins an apocalyptic novel like a good rapture, and such a breathtaking event is best conveyed by a memorable opening line. The first sentence in the book has to grab a reader and not let go until they've ponied up the $17.95 for the book, so yours should start something like:

> It was a bright cold day in April and the clocks were striking twelve as Jason Danger noticed that Duke Danger, his father, had suddenly lifted off the ground and ascended bodily into heaven.
>
> "What the hey is going on here?" Danger asked as he drove to his job as a handsome and rugged TV newsperson.

I don't know about you, but the Internet Theologian, for one, is hooked.

The next step is to follow Jason through the adventures of the Tribulation as he assembles a ragtag band of friends to resist the Antichrist, the Mark of the Beast, and, if licensing permits, Def Leppard.

You'll have to deal early with the Pretrib Character Conundrum, that is, explaining exactly why your hero didn't ascend into heaven along with his father and Don King. The key is to give him some kind of minor, regrettable flaw that's serious enough to keep him from the pearly gates but not so bad that it prevents the reader from

---

[15] Source: my friend Scott, a TV newsperson.

identifying with him. Here are some examples of good and bad flaws:

> *Voting Democrat once in college–good.*
> *Eating a bus full of schoolchildren–bad.*

You'll want to reserve your bus-eating for the main villain, who can be a shady industrialist, a charismatic political leader, the pope, or a trial lawyer. The villain, who will be the Antichrist, should also have a gamut[16] of toadies, temptresses, secular humanist advisers, and Bible scholars who will attempt to convince Jason Danger that he should be thinking about someone named Harpazo. Remember the secret that applies not just to writers of endtimes fiction, but to authors of every kind of book: padding is your friend.

Now, come up with a clever title (*Forecast: Apocalypse!*) and sit back while the royalty checks roll in.

Although the Internet Theologian has given you an excellent blueprint to Bible-based bestsellerdom, there is an important caveat to bear in mind. The prospective writer of endtimes fiction needs to remember one thing above and beyond the importance of a good title, a rugged TV newsperson as a main character, and that "Book of Revelation" does not have a final "s": although mainstream popular culture can provide you with important research materials and inspiration, under no circumstances should you attempt to create an endtimes novelization of popular ideas about the end of the world.

The distinction between Christian endtimes fiction (whether novels, films, puppet outreach ministry perfor-

---

[16] If you thought I was going to let up on the gamut jokes, you clearly haven't been paying attention.

mances, or small anonymous comic books handed to you by dazed homeless people) and secular endtimes fiction is critical. While space doesn't permit us to get into all the theoretical and theological subtleties, we can broadly summarize the distinction this way: secular people generally don't want the world to end, while Christians are kind of okay with it.

As an illustration, let's return, like so many crazy people have for centuries, to the Book of Revelation.

John the Divine has just gotten through describing what most people would reasonably describe as "a real bummer": dragons, beasts, lakes of fire, plagues, boiling seas, falling skies, gas prices soaring to five dollars a gallon. Descriptions like these are generally why secular people are leery about the end of the world; spectacular special effects aside, it sounds like a rather grim time.

John, however, concludes his narrative this way: "The one who testifies to these things says, 'Surely I am coming soon.' Amen. Come, Lord Jesus!"

In other words, "Come, Lord Jesus—and don't forget your boiling locust armies! Bring on the bleeding moon and the trumpets and those four disagreeable horsemen— truly, I say to you, I am stoked!"

This doesn't, of course, mean that Christians are looking forward to being stung[17] by swarms of locusts any more than your average person. It's just that for Christians, although the Book of Revelation has some pretty alarming passages, it turns out okay in the end. And, of course, there are believers who think Christians won't have to go through the locust stuff at all but will instead be

---

[17] Bitten? Slashed? Sued? What is it that locusts do, anyway?

trampolined up to heaven prior to all the unpleasantness.

The distinction between the Christian and secular views should be obvious. It's why, in secular treatments of the theme, the main characters are always trying to *stop* the end of the world, like the world is so great or something. This has never made sense to the Internet Theologian, particularly when the main characters are religious or even members of the clergy.

Wouldn't religious Christians sort of look forward to the end of the world? Granted, they may look forward to it only in the way a morbidly obese person looks forward to gastric bypass surgery; that is, it's more about joyous anticipation of what happens *after* the traumatic event. But Christians wouldn't be interested in forestalling the end of the world any more than our hypothetic stomach stapling candidate would push his or her doctor down an elevator shaft.

To the secular mind, though, the end of the world just means a heap of trouble, and that's why in countless movies, TV shows, and, for all I know, little Webcasts that teenagers watch on their phones, you have a group of heroes vainly trying to prevent the Spawn of Satan from getting into an elite nursery school, or something similar.

This disparity in views actually leads to some tension between the nonapocalyptic-novel-reading public and those who can't imagine a plane ride without taking along Jason Danger and Co.

Secular criticism seems to be that looking forward to the end of the world promotes a dangerous attitude bordering on fatalism: If there's war in the Middle East, that's okay, because that has to happen for the world to end. Also, we shouldn't worry about driving gas-guzzling trucklike vehicles that pollute the environment, because we can't really count on that many more generations before the Lord returns.[18] Plus, as some critics have pointed out, these books sow irrational fears about European politicians, bar codes, popes, and dragons.

These criticisms would be easier to take to heart if they applied to other bestselling novels. For example: Are our cities choked with shut-ins who, inspired by the novels of Stephen King, refuse to leave their homes lest they be murdered by a shape-shifting clown or a little girl who sets fires with her brain? No; at least, not outside Detroit. Have millions of Americans responded to the bestselling fantasias of Danielle Steele by leaving their husbands to run off with the passionate, impetuous stable boy?[19] No— in fact, just try and find an impetuous stable boy; they're surprisingly levelheaded and dispassionate.

The assumption is that Christians take the novels as more than just popular entertainment; beneath that assumption is the belief that Christians are far more gullible than nonbelievers, which is a hoot if you've ever talked to a Communist.

But there are criticisms of endtimes fiction that come from Christians themselves, and out of a sense of professional duty, it is to these criticisms that the Internet Theologian now turns.

---

[18] Although people born after, say, 1982 may have a hard time processing such a notion, this was an actual sentiment spoken in public by an important government official once. To find out which one, consult your local library. I think you'll be pleasantly surprised!

[19] Is that what people do in Danielle Steele novels?

DID ST. JOHN THE DIVINE
HAVE MOVIE RIGHTS IN MIND?

Beyond doctrinal questions about the biblical validity of the rapture and the usual objections from Catholics about how the bad guy is always either the pope or best friends with the pope, there's an unease with presenting religious doctrine as blockbuster entertainment.

As the prophet Amos put it somewhere in the Old Testament, "Alas for you who desire the day of the Lord! Why do you want the day of the Lord? It is darkness, not light."

To Christians in the Amos camp, the last days are not some kind of ultimate thrill to be anticipated like a spectator marinating in alcohol at a tailgate party for the homecoming game. They aren't the stuff of an action movie. The Tribulation is not something that will happen to other people. No, no; the "you" Amos is referring to means *everyone*.

The proper regard for such an awesome event, therefore, is not to write a thrilling action romp featuring a ruggedly handsome TV newsperson, but rather to reflect soberly on the words of the Bible and the teachings of wise Christians throughout history.

After judiciously considering this view, though, the Internet Theologian can easily boil it down to two simple words:

Sour grapes.

Boohoo, wary Christians! I'm playing the world's smallest e-violin in acknowledgment of your irrelevant complaints! "Popular novels trivialize the seriousness and gravity of eschatology," when translated by the Internet Theologian's Whiner-to-English Dictionary, sounds an awful lot like, "Waaah! I wish I had thought of writing novels like that first, instead of reading my Annotated Study Bible like a chump!"

Answer me this, gripers: if Jesus hadn't intended for the incredibly obtuse material in the Bible to be presented in an accessible and profitable way, why would he have told the Apostles, "Go forth, and bring my teachings to all nations in the form of gripping narrative dramas populated by leggy temptresses and two-fisted TV weathermen?"[20]

In fact, this treatment could be fruitful and rewarding for other, less dragon-prone biblical texts. Who wouldn't enjoy a novelization of the Book of Acts, set in present-day Los Angeles, featuring Paul as a hard-bitten private eye and Luke as his wisecracking sidekick? And if, instead of debating James and Peter at Jerusalem over the question of Gentile converts, what if they had a crazy, no-rules, cross-country car race from New York City to San Francisco? *That* would certainly make the vagaries of first-century Jewish theological controversy relevant to a modern audience. And think of the merchandising tie-ins!

The point is, in today's workaday world, with distractions ranging from ten-hour shifts to truly excellent cable television programming, no one has the time or the inclination to read the Bible, not even the allegedly modern translation of the New Revised Standard Version.[21] If Christians really want people to avoid slipping below the biblical literacy of the average Def Leppard fan, they'll wholeheartedly support a gamut[22] of popular nov-

---

[20] Source: a crude forgery.

[21] For a "modern" version, it's still remarkably full of "hillocks" and "whole burnt offerings" and "vineyards." Uh, hello? It's the twenty-first century. Can we possibly get some iPods in this thing?

[22] Last one.

elizations, using the successful endtimes versions as their model.

After all, the goal is to get people interested in the Bible while acknowledging that the likelihood of their actually reading it is only slightly greater than the chance that Hamas and the Israeli Defense Force will spontaneously break into a dazzling rendition of "Zing! Went the Strings of My Heart" on the outskirts of Gaza.

It's a simple equation: More endtimes novels equals more vaguely biblically aware people in the population. And that's an outcome all the various factions—pretribulationist, midtribulationist, and Shiite alike—can agree on.

Oh, and by the way: If I happen by the bookstore in a few months and see a new bestselling endtimes novel featuring a rugged TV newsperson named Jason Danger, the next time you'll see the Internet Theologian will be in court.

CONCLUSION

THE FURTHER ADVENTURES OF JESUS

When Christianity began nearly two thousand years ago, its earliest adherents hardly could have imagined the shapes their faith would take at the dawn of the twenty-first century. The distance from small, persecuted Jewish sect to world-straddling megafaith is vast. And yet, with the advantage of hindsight — perhaps the greatest tool available to the Internet Theologian — we can see that what we bemoan or celebrate as distant from the origins of Christianity is not, in fact, quite so foreign after all.

Popular culture is the great controversy of our era's Christianity, our version of the first-century argument about Gentile conversion, perhaps, or of the great sixteenth-century controversy about who was smarter, Luther or the pope. Christians in America today grapple with the question of whether to engage with the larger culture and, if they should, to what degree? How far is too far? How much engagement is too much? When does the bearded, guitar-strumming hippie pastor shade over into the foul-mouthed hip hop Mass?

Christians today imagine that these controversies are unique to our time. A corresponding lament is that, while Christians in earlier times certainly had their own worries,[1] the faith was simpler, purer, less tainted by the secular world. Today's Christians, beset by evangelistic skateboarders, *What Would Jesus Do?* booklets about file sharing, and all-expenses paid trips to Bible-themed amusement parks, posit the past as an innocent golden age into which the concerns and complexities of the present never intruded.

As the Internet Theologian has tried to show — both in this volume and in countless exasperated posts in comment boxes throughout cyberspace — this view is profoundly mistaken. In fact, today's grappling over questions of diluting the faith through the media of popular culture is as old as Christianity itself.

Early Christians fretted over the extent to which they should blend their faith with Greek philosophy and classical writing — the popular culture of their day. Granted, it was extremely boring popular culture,[2] but then, you can't really blame them; they were living centuries before the invention of TiVo.

Succeeding controversies in the Church revolved around other aspects of popular culture: Arius used sea chanteys to spread the heretical doctrine of Arianism, which claimed that Jesus was German; the iconoclasm controversy that gripped the Church for centuries focused on a popular art form;[3] and the Protestant Reformation

---

[1] For example, public execution by lions.

[2] Particularly Aristotle.

[3] Today, "iconoclast" is a term of praise for, say, a corporate executive who comes up with a new way to market tacos, but historically, the iconoclasts were tremendous drips.

began with Martin Luther's bold act of graffiti. So, clearly, throughout its history, Christianity has been anything but immune to doctrinal clashes with the broader culture.

But today's whiny Christians are correct in asserting that contemporary controversies differ significantly in some ways from those which came before. To begin with, starting in about the fifth century, popular culture was synonymous with Christian culture, except in Northern Europe, where the pagans were busy inventing Christmas, Halloween, Mother's Day, and the World Series of Poker. The distinctions between classical culture and Christian culture that tormented early Christians had largely vanished: all culture was seen as a single mosaic celebrating the glory of the Creator. That's why, for example, you'd get mystery plays performed in churches that mostly revolved around farting, foul-mouthed devil characters, and no one batted an eyelash.

No one thought to question whether a four-hour miracle play that involved a tremendous amount of cross-dressing was trivializing the faith; I mean, it was performed in church. If anyone had raised such objections at the time, they'd either be laughed out of the room or trampled to death by deranged Flemish peasants.[4]

Like so much else in history, this all began to go wrong during the Renaissance. The bored Italian dandies who invented that short-lived craze "discovered" the Greek and Latin classics and once again began to view secular culture and sacred culture as distinct spheres. Granted, they generally saw the two as compatible, but it wasn't long before other, nuttier Europeans picked up that ball and ran.

---

[4] Which was actually the prescribed form of capital punishment in parts of Europe until well into the 1950s.

The Renaissance was so popular that they produced a sequel, Renaissance II: The Enlightenment, and by then the separation of religious and secular culture had become characterized by bitter enmity. The bewigged Frenchmen who cooked up Renaissance II were set on repudiating not just religious culture but Christianity in general, a project that culminated in the French Revolution (which closed shortly after receiving terrible reviews).

What was different now, though, was that Christians themselves had accepted the idea that not only were sacred and secular culture separate, but they were necessarily antagonistic. In fairness, many Christians developed this thesis while being executed by rampaging mobs of *sans culottes*,[5] when it probably seemed quite plausible.

Since that early modern period, known to historians as "The Era of Insane, Syphilitic Monarchs," the gulf between popular culture and Christianity grew ever wider until, in the early twentieth century, many Christians could be anathematized by their churches simply for the act of accidentally seeing a movie poster out of the corner of their eye. Christians had at last returned to the perspective of the earliest members of their church: the world was irredeemably corrupt and doomed, and the only thing for Christians to do was to wait for the return of Jesus and possibly get devoured by lions. In the absence of significant threats of lion-related devourings in the twentieth century, many Christians became even more despondent.

Then, something changed. Perhaps it was the popularity of Christian novels like *Quo Vadis?*, *Ben Hur*, and *The Valley of the Dolls*. Perhaps it was the dawning recognition that popular culture was the way the world spoke to itself

---

[5] A French term indicating people who work themselves into a fury by filling their trousers with sand.

in the twentieth century and that any viable worldview would do well to join the conversation. Perhaps it was the dulcet tones of Pat Boone. At any rate, as the modern age wore on, Christians stopped fighting against popular culture and began adapting it to suit their own needs.

The idea that a series of explicitly Christian novels depicting the end of the world would be the bestselling books in the country would have seemed preposterous in 1920; in the early twenty-first century, that's exactly what happened. Anyone trying to sell Hollywood back in 1930 on the idea that a film about Christ's crucifixion acted entirely in Latin, Hebrew, and Aramaic could be a blockbuster would be laughed out of the building and then trampled to death by Flemish peasants. And yet *The Passion of the Christ* was one of the top-grossing films of 2004. As recently as 1970, the notion of Christian rock would have been greeted with incredulous scorn. And yet that very notion has created today an industry that annually takes in roughly twelve squintillion dollars.[6] Clearly, the Christians who shrank from the realm of popular culture in decades past have now come to claim their dual inheritance as both believers and Americans who watch an average of eight hours of television per day.

This entrance of faith into the cultural realm, though, has not been without controversy. Christians intuitively grasp that participation in the broader cultural conversation is a two-way street — Christians influence the culture, but the culture also influences Christianity.

Nowhere is this influence more obvious than in the mushrooming world of Bible publishing. Everyone knows the Bible is the bestselling book of all time, trouncing not

---

[6] Note to editor: I will get the real number before this goes to press.

only *Harry Potter* and *The Da Vinci Code*, but also absolutely laying waste to hoity-toity favorites like James Joyce's *Ulysses*. But an even more eye-opening truth is that the Bible is the bestselling book of the year, every year. Annually, Americans buy about twenty-five million Bibles, spending roughly half a billion dollars to do so.[7] That's a lot of Bibles, especially when you consider the Gideons just hand the thing out for free all over the country. Either Americans are suckers, they're inexcusably careless with their Bibles and in constant need of replacements, or there's a spiritual hunger being satisfied by constantly new versions.

That's the real secret of the Bible industry: Americans aren't buying twenty-five million study copies of the New Revised Standard Version.[8] They are buying Bibles sold to them as syntheses of sacred Scripture and popular culture. Indeed, Bible publishing insiders predict that, if current trends persist, by the year 2012 all editions of the Bible published in America will contain either the words "Teen," "Women's," or "X-Treme" in their titles.

Thoughtful Christians, when faced with this phenomenon, quite naturally ask the obvious questions: How can I horn in on this action? And how long will it take me to rush my X-Treme Teen's Skateboarding Biblezine for Women onto the market?

A smaller, more excitable group of Christians, though, is asking different questions. They're wondering whether people are buying these Bibles because they're the word

---

[7] These facts come from the December 18, 2006 issue of the *New Yorker*. That's right: the Internet Theologian reads the *New Yorker*. He also knows how to match wine with food. Can't handle a cosmopolitan Internet Theologian? Tough.

[8] Thank goodness for that. 2,337 pages!

of God, or because of their enticing packaging, summarizations, and copious illustrations, all of which can serve to spread the false message that the Bible is an easy document to grasp and can be assimilated as no more than a lifestyle accessory.

And although these questions are put forth by the sort of worrywart killjoys who try to ruin Christmas by wringing their hands over toys that are choking hazards or who can't let Columbus Day go by without bringing up genocide, they are valid inquiries.

In Christianity, the Bible sits at the heart of the faith. If the Bible can be trivialized, appropriated by culture, fashioned into just another product on the marketplace, what chance does Christianity's core message stand of remaining untarnished by its pop culture translations?

Luckily for us, we will be dead long before the answers to these questions become clear. So if it turns out that popular culture does inflict significant distortion on Christianity, well, that's something for our children to worry about! After all, we can't fight all their battles for them. Trust me: they'll thank us for the valuable growth experience.

In the meantime, we're left with the current phenomenon of Christianity and popular culture uniting like they have at no time since the farting devils of the miracle plays capered across cathedrals throughout Western Europe. It's somehow unsatisfying simply to sit back and catalogue current trends in Christianity, though. At the backs of our minds, there's a constant desire to know more, to look a little further down the road and glimpse what might lay in wait for us.

As proven conclusively in this volume, the Internet Theologian is unsurpassed when it comes to digesting centuries of complex history and theology and producing a cogent and informative summation of our current situation and how we got here. But my diligent research on the myriad intersections between Christianity and popular culture also allows me to offer confidently some predictions about what the future holds.

Who says the future cannot be known?[9]

1 CHRISTIAN NETWORKING WEB SITES. As you probably know if you read the police blotter in your local paper, MySpace is the social networking Web site that has taken the world by storm. It not only allows people to meet "face to face" with other users all around the world, it's revolutionized the way lousy bands and mediocre stand-up comics alike ply their trades. With such runaway success—as of this writing, 340 million Americans currently have a MySpace account[10]—can a Christian version be far behind? So far, Christians are wary of the site, because these days it's used primarily to stalk exes and as a means for lonely perverts to ogle young girls. It can't be long before there's a ChristSpace or similar social network for Christians looking for the slightly alienating feel of connecting with people via a publicly hosted computer page but also wanting to make sure they don't get five e-mails a day from girls soliciting business for their webcam sites.

2 CHRISTIAN HORROR MOVIES. "Wait a minute," you're probably saying. "Aren't there plenty of Christian

---

[9] Jesus, according to Mark 13:32. However, many scholars believe he was here referring specifically to World Series predictions.

[10] Source: a typo.

horror movies out there already, such as *The Exorcist*, *The Omen*, and those movies starring the sidekick from *Charles in Charge*?" Close, except you're completely wrong. Those movies are examples of Hollywood screenwriters with little grasp of genuine theology importing a few concepts into formulaic monsters vs. decent people scripts, wrenching them out of context, and billing each as a chilling masterpiece with spiritual implications. What's going to happen soon is a flowering of horror movies made by Christians for the increasingly large Christian moviegoing demographic. I'm talking about horror movies in which, say, a demon-possessed maniac stalks a local Christian skate park or a werewolf is stopped from shredding a shipment of teen study Bibles by a plucky coed with a WWJD bracelet.

3   **CHRISTIAN GOSSIP.** One of the real growth industries in America today is celebrity gossip: details about the marriages, divorces, and bizarre adoptions of the famous are routinely used as hard newsbreaks. The gossip column is no longer confined to the ghettos of the tabloids and the glossy magazines in supermarket checkout aisles. The day is rapidly approaching when this gossip-hunger will make its way to the Christian media. Brace yourself for blurry paparazzi photos of Christian celebrities dozing off in church or blind items about a famous pastor taking the Lord's name in vain after whacking his thumb with a hammer while trying to hang a Thomas Kinkade painting in his office. This trend may show an ugly side, too, as unscrupulous gossipmongers begin "outing" celebrities as hardcore pretribulationists. And get ready for

a barrage of stories about Christian celebs who have "lusted in their hearts."

4 **BIBLE SEQUELS.** At first blush, this seems the least plausible item on the list of that which is yet to come. Christians, after all, have been pretty content with the first two Bibles for nearly 1,700 years now. It would be the height of presumption to start writing sequels, especially when you consider that even the longest-lived Apostle has likely been dead for more than 1,900 years. But think about it for a second: Hollywood's big summer blockbusters are almost invariably remakes and sequels. Indeed, the American appetite for sequels is at its most voracious since the public demanded—and got—*Rambo III*. A Bible III would do incredible business. Just look at the Mormons—they've got a sequel to the Bible, and they're doing terrific. They have a whole state and a successful NBA franchise, for crying out loud. And think about the success of the *Harry Potter* franchise. And it's not like the sequel would have to pick up where the New Testament leaves off.[11] Why, there could even be a series of prequels instead of sequels, like with the *Star Wars* trilogy, except hopefully less disappointing. Who wouldn't thrill over *The Adventures of Teen Jesus*? Or maybe there could be a gritty, dark, HBO-style prequel following Paul's experiences as Saul of Tarsus, persecutor of Christians. The point is that the Bible leaves a lot of stuff out, and there are

---

[11] A difficult task, since the New Testament concludes with the end of the world. Still, I think there's room for an Escape From New York-type sequel in which a ragtag group of historical scoundrels team up and try to break out of hell.

areas which could be profitably shaded in by a well-made sequel or two. (And don't bother protesting that you'd never stand for it; *it's already happening.*)

5 YET MORE COLORFUL BRACELETS. When Lance Armstrong started encouraging people to wear yellow bracelets for, I believe, postal awareness, he started a trend which Americans have embraced like none other since legal reforms made it even easier to file frivolous lawsuits. Today, you can hardly buy groceries without being solicited a donation in exchange for a rubber bracelet that somehow, by virtue of your wearing it, fights against a vaguely defined social evil, like illiteracy or Dutch Elm disease. Naturally, there are already Christian varieties, many of which are emblazoned with the initials WWJD, but don't be fooled into thinking the bracelets stop there. Down the road, you're going to see bracelets promoting Bible literacy, abstinence until marriage, Trinitarianism, partisanship for particular Bible translations, opposition to Dynamic Modalism, and, in a postmodern coup de grace, a colorful Christian wristband promoting awareness of other colorful Christian wristbands. Upon manufacture of the last of these, however, the universe may implode. Perhaps this is a small price to pay for conceptual purity.

No matter what, it's clear that in the foreseeable future, Christianity and popular culture will remain close allies, although the creative tension that currently exists between them can be expected to get more noticeable. Christianity will seek to leave a lasting mark on popular consciousness, while popular culture will seek to continue selling Christians a bunch of T-shirts emblazoned with gimmicky slogans. We may never fully resolve this tension, but then, maybe it's better that way: the frisson keeps both Christianity and mass culture sharp, innovative, and—best of all—completely incomprehensible to the average observer.

The future looks bright for the Internet Theologian. America's fascination with Christianity seems to be in inverse proportion to its comprehension of the faith; as religion becomes a topic of analysis and concern among even the contentedly godless, it seems the most basic facts about faith are completely forgotten in the rush to post a truly scathing blog entry. Ignorance fuels insult, and before long public discourse comes to resemble what the Bible calls "a tale told by an idiot—full of sound and fury, signifying absolutely zippo."

And so, with all due respect to Dom DiMaggio, a nation turns its lonely eyes to *me*, and to others like me, dedicated independent scholars who rely on nothing more than finely honed common sense and a high-speed Internet connection in order to ferret out the complex, fascinating creature we call Truth.

In these confusing, tumultuous times, the daily skirmishes between religion and popular culture are crying out for a referee, and the Internet Theologian is wearing black and white stripes and blowing a whistle.

After all, isn't that how the Scriptures themselves foretold it? A prophet is without honor in his own country without at least a T1 connection, or something? I'm paraphrasing. Anyway, the point is, Jesus said, "Lead my sheep": and I'm here to bring you woolly critters to safe pastures.

With such a lofty image in our minds, there can be no better way to end this treatise than with the following prophetic quotation from the book of Ezekiel:

"When, in the course of human events, it becomes necessary not to praise Caesar, but to bury him, two roads diverged in a wood and I took the one less traveled by. We hold these truths to be self-evident: I think, therefore I am. Do unto others. I can call you Betty and Betty, when you call me, you can call me Al."[12]

And the people said, Amen.

---

[12] Source: an old college notebook rendered illegible by a Dr. Pepper spill.